NEW CLASSICAL MUSIC

GORDON KERRY is a classical composer whose works are regularly performed and broadcast in Australia, Europe and the USA. A widely published writer on music generally, he was a critic for the *Sydney Morning Herald* in the late 1990s, contributes occasional features (including book reviews) to publications such as *The Australian*, *The Australian Financial Review* and *24 Hours*, and has contributed to books on Australian music issued by the Australian Music Centre and Ashgate Press. He lives on a hill in Victoria and maintains a website at <www.gordonkerry.com>.

NEW CLASSICAL MUSIC

COMPOSING AUSTRALIA

Gordon Kerry

Contents

Acknowledgments

There are, as ever, many people to thank and I apologise for any sins of omission.

Roger Covell and Richard Toop both gave generously of their time and wisdom at the project's commencement; Graeme Skinner and Andrew Yencken read the final drafts and made invaluable suggestions for improvement, while along the way, Gordon Kalton Williams was a wonderful sounding-board, editor and devil's advocate. The Australian Music Centre's director, John Davis, shared advice, and as-yet unpublished material with me, while Judith Foster patiently kept me supplied with recordings, scores and books from the library's collection as did Leisa Radford from the library of Symphony Australia. Robert Patterson and Natalie Shea generously allowed me access to ABC Classics CDs, as did Belinda Webster for Tall Poppies Records, while Lorna Lander and Gregory Dobbs at the Australian Music Unit of ABC

Classic FM made it possible for me to hear many archival recordings made for broadcast. Michael Pedersen and Emma Williams (Opera Australia), Anne Frankenberg (Victoria Opera), Margaret Moore and Bernie Heard (Sydney Symphony Orchestra), Phillip Sametz and Katherine Kerezsi (Melbourne Symphony Orchestra), Janine Kyle (Sydney Dance Company), Vincent Plush (National Film and Sound Archive), Helen Champion (Victorian Department of Education), Jonathon Bird (Universal Music), Philip McCarthy (Boosey and Hawkes), Gill Graham (Chesters) and Diane Parks (ABC Magazines) were marvellously responsive to requests for information, program material, permissions and photographs, as were Ann Morgan, Wayne Stuart and Pattie Benjamin. Richard Letts (Music Council of Australia) and Douglas Horton (ChamberMade) allowed me to try out certain ideas in their publications.

I am grateful for the opportunity to use beautiful images by Bridget Elliot, Christabelle Baranay, Dean Golja, Greg Devine, Branco Gaica, Kiren Chang and Brian Blanchflower. My thanks also to the team at UNSW Press, especially Elspeth Menzies who commissioned the book, Chantal Gibbs who managed it and me, managing editor Heather Cam, Dieter Bajzek who handled the production of the CD and the eagle-eyed Kerrie Mann who edited the final copy. Ute Bierbaumer, Marena Manzoufas, Kate Lidbetter, Terry Stokes, Stephen Wedlick, Siobhan Lenihan, Carolyn Masel and Joseph Toltz offered, sometimes inadvertently, wise counsel.

Finally, and most importantly, thanks to my composer colleagues: not just those who provided me with scores, recordings and other information but all who have contributed to the vibrant culture of Australian music today.

Introduction

'There we held out in the bitterest cold from half-past six to half-past ten and experienced the fact that one can easily have too much of a good — and even more of a strong — thing.'

Sound familiar? Probably, if you've attended many contemporary music concerts over the last few decades. If so, you'll know the drill. You head out on a cold evening early in the week arriving at some theatre which is free that night, or maybe a church with furniture designed to keep Calvinist backs straight. The audience is small and contains many people whom you would, under normal circumstances, take pains to avoid. Groups of unconventionally matched instrumentalists take their places on stage (requiring changes of set-up which take almost as much time as the actual music does to play) and perform works with titles which are either suggestive monosyllables or vaguely, you know, 'scientific'. And at interval you'll be lucky if you can find a cube of stale cheese and a plastic cup of warm white wine. I've been there – lots.

But the quotation with which I began was not from one of our contemporaries. It comes from a letter by one Johann Friedrich Reichardt[1] who, one cold winter night in 1808, had sat through a concert which included Beethoven's Fourth and Fifth Symphonies, the Choral Fantasia, much of the Mass in C and one or two other things like the Fourth Piano Concerto. If I may make the obvious point, this listener was grumpy at the discomfort (largely Beethoven's fault, as he hadn't paid to have the hall heated), but he knew the value of the music he had heard – for the first time – and the value of supporting it. Now by no means all of the music performed in contemporary music concerts will attain the cultural status of any work of Beethoven's. But some might, and on those unpromising-seeming occasions it is possible to have a transcendental musical experience. The composers and performers who take the trouble to present their work to any public do so because they believe it to be important. And the small audience for a hard-edged contemporary show might just include a composer who is inspired by the music, an administrator who goes into bat for it, a critic who will try eloquently to interpret the music. It has been my privilege to be, at one time or another, each of those people, and it is my hope that in this book you'll feel some of the enthusiasm I have for Australian music.

This book is about notated western art music for acoustic instruments. Occasionally I have referred to composers' radiophonic works, or others outside the square if doing so illuminates the discussion of a particular piece; it has meant though that I haven't addressed sound art, or indeed fine composers like Roger Dean and David Chesworth who work principally in electro-acoustic media. I have chosen to divide it into themes, rather than styles or genres. Each theme is the subject of a general essay, and then I have chosen a few works as 'case studies' to illustrate the theme in detail. Any such scheme is arbitrary – any number of the works discussed here fit into more than one of the thematic categories. But it was a way of demonstrating that differences of style are superficial: I regard each work that I discuss as 'well made', and that was my sole criterion. Given the relatively abundant documentation of Australian music since 1967 and especially in the 1970s, I have chosen to focus on work from around 1979 to the present day.

Things, as I say, have changed in the last 20 years. Contemporary music is much more a feature of mainstream concert programming than it was, and is rightly regarded as a proper aspect of music education. Moreover, in Australia the range of styles, voices and aesthetics that coexist more or less peacefully is huge. As I hope to demonstrate in this book there are many works of enormous quality; naturally, in a work of this size it has only been possible to discuss a fragment of what's out there. If this book is of any use it will be in encouraging readers to go exploring. Most composers mentioned here have websites; these can be found with any search engine or by visiting the Australian Music Centre online (<www.amcoz.com.au>). And anyone can join the AMC: for a modest subscription you have access to recordings and scores and can be kept up to date with performances of new works. Those works, sadly many which are not available on commercial recordings, may nonetheless be held by ABC Classic FM or the Music Broadcasting Society (MBS) in your capital city, and you can always request that they be played.

Like any composer and critic I have acquired a precious store of insults. I have been called 'misogynist', 'the devil in Australian music' and a 'musicological monarchist' (no, I don't know either) – all by people mentioned in these pages (my next book will be called *Settling Scores*). It's the 'musicological' that really stings. I am not a musicologist and this is not a work of academic scholarship; nor does it have any pretentions to being encyclopaedic. I have tried to place composers and works in historical and aesthetic contexts, to give a sense of how certain works sound, and to convey why these works inspire me. I have tried to keep the inevitable technical discussion to a minimum; if it seems baffling, take it as a challenge: go out and listen to the piece.

Chapter 1

40 Years On

In 1967 Roger Covell published his *Australia's Music: Themes of a New Society*. It might not have been the first time Australian music had been treated seriously in print, but it was certainly the first comprehensive study of music in Australia since white settlement. Covell's account of the story of western music in this country takes us from soldiers' marches through quadrilles and parlour songs to the 1960s, when Australian composers regained a sense of contemporaneity, and it charts the rise of institutions which to a great extent made that possible. Covell was no voice crying in the wilderness, though, in the sense that the late sixties was a time in which serious discussion of the arts was vibrant. Graeme Skinner's recent *Peter Sculthorpe: The Making of an Australian Composer* offers a fascinating picture of the documentation of new music through serious journalism – in the daily newspapers. Many of those critics were European émigrés who might have felt that music's essential role in civilised life was not as well understood here as in Europe. Though born in Australia, Covell was one of those critics, and his book was indicative of a newly pervasive interest in the contemporary arts in this country.

In music we can point to the rise of John Hopkins as the ABC's Director of Music from 1963 and his active support of new works on radio and in the concert hall; Musica Viva Australia began commissioning in 1966. There was a major increase in tertiary music education: over the decade from 1965, younger universities like Monash, La Trobe and New South Wales (the latter thanks to Roger Covell) established music departments while the Canberra School of Music opened in 1965 and the Victorian College of the Arts, with Hopkins as its founding director, began in 1974. Important composers took teaching posts at some of these institutions, raising composition's status. Hand in hand with this was a sense that musicology could legitimately turn its sights on Australian music. Frank Callaway and David Tunley, based at the University of Western Australia, edited the valuable collection *Australian Composition in the Twentieth Century* in 1978, the same year that Andrew McCredie took up a chair of musicology at the University of Adelaide. Both within and outside the academies, writing about Australian music has since prospered in the work of Thérèse Radic, Alison Gyger, Malcolm Gillies and others. And in Sydney in 1973 they finally opened the Opera House. (The Sydney Opera House is of course a powerful symbol of the role of the arts in Australia, and the saga of its getting built at all is a salutary reminder about the uneasy relationship of art and power.) Other cities likewise engaged in ambitious programs of building in the 1970s, producing the Adelaide Festival Centre, Perth Concert Hall, Melbourne Concert (now Hamer) Hall and, a little later, the Queensland Performing Arts Centre.

The 1970s saw a number of changes, some of which were foreshadowed in Covell's book. He had rightly criticised the ABC for not having the equivalent of a Third Program (now BBC Radio 3) devoted to classical music; the rise of stereo FM broadcasting in the 1970s, and the enthusiasm with which community-based music broadcasting societies took up licences in various capital cities, prodded the ABC into founding what is now its Classic FM network. Federal government support for the arts increased dramatically during the prime ministerships of Harold Holt and John Gorton, and this was much increased in the new decade with the election of the Whitlam Government. The Australian Council for the Arts was established in 1968 but became the Australia Council by an Act of Parliament in 1975: instead of committees which advised on the use of discretionary funding by government ministers, the Council was a statutory body that enshrined the principle of 'arms length' funding and peer assessment. It didn't of course take the politics out of funding – far from it – but it did, perhaps, protect against undue partisan influence on the arts.

People started to come home. Composers like Don Banks and Peggy Glanville-Hicks returned to Australia after long periods of expatriation. Glanville-Hicks, admittedly, was in seriously ill-health so her activities were confined to some lecturing, but on her death in 1990 she bequeathed her home in Sydney's Paddington as a haven for composers. Banks returned in 1972 to take up a fellowship in creative arts in Canberra, and the following year accepted the prime minister's invitation to chair the Music Board of the Australian Council for the Arts. Banks' health suffered too, as he battled cancer for several years while working tirelessly to build a sustainable structure for new music in this country. He was aided in this by a number of people, such as Kenneth Tribe, a Sydney lawyer whose service to the Australia Council and Musica Viva Australia – to name but two organisations – was of immense value to Australian culture over a half-century. Another expatriate, James Murdoch, returned to Australia in 1972 after establishing a successful business as the London agent for composers Peter Maxwell Davies and Harrison Birtwistle, ensembles like The Fires of London and pianists Roger Woodward and Paul Crossley. Back in Australia, Murdoch acted as consultant to the Music Board of the Australian Council for the Arts, and in that capacity fought for the establishment of the Australian Music Centre as a national service and information organisation; he became that institution's founding director. He was also behind some of the most important documentation of Australian music, notably in his books, *Australia's Contemporary Composers* and *A Handbook of Australian Music* (he has more recently published a biography of Peggy Glanville-Hicks) and as the artistic director of the multi-volume *Australian Festival of Music* series of LP records, an invaluable document of the rise of new music in this country.

Among those who returned were Keith Humble, who was a co-founder of the Australian Contemporary Music Ensemble, one of the many new-music ensembles that were established at this time. ACME was founded in 1975 as one of the flagship companies supported by the Music Board. The previous year the Synergy Percussion ensemble was founded; in 1976 the Seymour Group came into existence under the artistic direction of the indefatigable composer, broadcaster and facilitator Vincent Plush. Originally housed in the University of Sydney's Seymour Theatre Centre, and enjoying nothing like the funding of ACME, the Seymour Group stayed in existence for three decades. In 1978 Melbourne's Astra Chamber Music Society appointed composer John McCaughey as its artistic director, inaugurating an era (still going) devoted to fascinating combinations of historic and new work; similarly, the University of NSW agreed in 1980 to support the creation of the Australia Ensemble, a flexible ensemble also devoted to both traditional and newly composed music. Out of the ashes of ACME's demise in 1979 was born the legendary Flederman, which over its ten-year life performed Australian music throughout the world, commissioning nearly 80 works. Since the late 1970s a huge number of ensembles have come and gone; they continue to form and dissolve according to the enthusiasms of their founders and their ability to stay financially secure. Ensembles more recently formed, and still standing, include several founded by or associated with particular composers. David Pye's Nova Ensemble began life in Perth in 1983 and has included among its performers the composers Cathie Travers, Iain Grandage and Ross Bolleter; in 1986 the Elision Ensemble was founded by Daryl Buckley in Melbourne and soon became the pre-eminent ensemble for 'pointy end' new music from both Australia and

Synergy Percussion. Photo by Bridget Elliot.

abroad (composer Liza Lim in particular has benefited from Elision's enthusiasm and competence); Robert Davidson founded Topology in Brisbane in 1997.

Performance opportunities have grown exponentially over the last four decades with the establishment of national and state opera companies, and companies like Melbourne's ChamberMade dedicated to new music theatre. Under the umbrella of the ABC until very recently, the state symphony orchestras maintained a commitment to new works; whether in their now devolved state they will be able to balance that commitment with a need to balance their budgets remains to be seen.

And people came to visit. As we'll see, a number of important composers came here from elsewhere, in several cases expecting to stay only a short time but settling here only to change and be changed by the Australian musical climate. Among those who did come for brief but influential periods was Peter Maxwell Davies. In 1972 Davies wrote the Foreword to his friend James Murdoch's *Australia's Contemporary Composers*, in which he said that we were witnessing 'the early struggles of something great'.[1] I hope this book proves him right.

Chapter 2

40 000 Years On

People have been singing and dancing to music here for some 40 000 years. The Aboriginal peoples of Australia were almost exclusively hunter-gatherers and with little by way of material possessions or wants developed an extremely complex spirituality which was expressed in ritual song and dance. These are not performances or retelling of mythical stories: they are, for the traditional Aboriginal, a means of bringing the eternal world of spirit ancestors into the present. What is misleadingly called 'the Dreaming' isn't a bunch of 'once upon a time' stories; it's a way of understanding the ongoing and eternal process of creation of the landscape, plants, animals and people. Rituals and songs are specific to particular sites, and these songs are 'owned' by a particular individual or groups of people associated with that place. So we can assume that music in the form of song and rhythmic accompaniment has been part of Australian life for a very long time.

Australia was isolated, but not completely. Traders from Macassar and even China appear to have visited the northern coast for trade. In the seventeenth century a couple of Dutch and British sailors made landfall on the north-west coast but, faced with a flat desert stretching as far as the eye could see, they went away again leaving New Holland, as they called it, for the people that one described as the 'miserablest in the world'.[1] Dutch, Spanish, French and British sailors sought out the fabled Great South Land during the eighteenth century and found bits of it – or thought they did – but it was the voyage of James Cook, who mapped the eastern coast of Australia, calling it New South Wales, in 1770 that was a turning point, especially when King George III carelessly lost the American colonies and needed somewhere else to transport the huge number of convicts – many convicted of stealing food – under which the British penal system strained.

So in 1788 the First Fleet, full of convicts and troopers, arrived at what Cook had called Botany Bay, but soon established the new colony about 500 metres from where the Sydney Opera House now stands on Sydney Harbour. And soon after, as Roger Covell describes in *Australia's Music*, we have the first instance of western music played on Australian soil – characteristically, a trooper who had breached discipline was frog-marched out of the camp and given a good flogging to the tune of *The Rogues' March* played on fife and drum.

To the first settlers, colonial Sydney Town must have seemed marooned between the Pacific Ocean and the Blue Mountains which present an unbroken line of escarpments to the west. Eventually some white explorers found a way over them and 'discovered' an immense plain ideal for raising sheep and cattle. The whaling industry contributed immensely to the development of towns like Sydney, Hobart in Tasmania and Albany in Western Australia. The gold rushes of the 1850s in the colonies of NSW and Victoria brought a wave of immigration from California, Europe and China and left in their wake Victorian boom towns like Melbourne. This in turn had people seeking to replicate a genteel lifestyle, so much so that a French traveller, quoted by Covell, remarked that there were more pianos per head of population in Australia in the later nineteenth century than in France. Earlier in the century the quadrille enjoyed a vogue, and while none were written in Australia, they were repackaged with 'aboriginal' names (and a French definite article) like *La Illawarra* and my favourite, *La Bong Bong*. In the 1980s Richard Meale (born 1932) used some of these to evoke the colonial setting of his opera *Voss*, after the novel by Patrick White about a fictional German explorer.

With pianos, of course, came piano teachers, and with teachers, the rise of music schools and conservatoriums. This mirrored the rapid transformation of Australia into an essentially urban, middle-class society in the wake of the late-nineteenth-century boom, and it produced composers. Many of these have fallen into obscurity – posterity often gets it right – although Larry Sitsky, in researching his recent *Australian Piano Music of the Twentieth Century*, was delighted to discover a small but significant body of innovative and original music from the first half of the twentieth century in the work of Raymond Hanson (1913–1976), Roy Agnew (1891–1944) and others. Moreover, just as South Australia and New Zealand led the world in women's suffrage, the Antipodes established a long tradition of composers who were women. They simply got down and wrote the music that needed to be written for teaching young performers as well as more substantial works. The mid-twentieth century produced some who are still household names (in households where members do AMEB (Australian Music Education Board) exams, at least): Miriam Hyde (1913–2005), Dulcie Holland (1913–2000), Esther Rofe (1904–2000). So while it's easy to fall into the trap of writing a history of 'Great Composers', there are of course many people of less public achievement who helped pave the way.

In colonial and early twentieth century Australia, music was largely a domestic art – hence the ubiquity of the piano. But hand in hand with that went a higher level of musical literacy in the general population than obtains now that music is so easily experienced in concert or on radio or recording. Colonial cities had their fair share of theatres, and there were performances of, for instance, early Wagner operas within a decent interval after their European premieres. Who knows how they sounded, of course, but we know from a letter from the composer that he was delighted that his work was being performed here – though he wished, interestingly and importantly, that it had been sung in English.[2] Theatre orchestras, then, existed in some form here in the nineteenth century; symphony orchestras of varying sizes and qualities were formed in the different cities – as long ago as 1906 in Melbourne – and these were given a degree of stability by being brought under the umbrella of the Australian Broadcasting Commission (the ABC), as it then was, in the 1940s.

So it wasn't a complete cultural desert, though as the twentieth century progressed we continued to import our major institutional figures and conductors, and send our more promising students to study abroad. Composers like Peggy Glanville-Hicks (1912–1990) and Margaret Sutherland (1897–1984) studied at the Royal College of Music in London, and Peter Sculthorpe (born 1929) many years later made the statutory pilgrimage to the United Kingdom. Others went to Germany or the United States. Sculthorpe's student, and my teacher, Barry Conyngham (born 1944) was the subject of a front page article in the *Sydney Morning Herald* in 1970 because he announced that his Churchill Fellowship would take him, not to England or Germany or the USA, but to Tokyo where he studied with the late Tōru Takemitsu. Clearly, things had changed.

‿

The composer Alfred Hill (1870–1960) was prolific; though not wildly individual, he nonetheless was very important to the development of music in both Australia and New Zealand. Born in Melbourne, raised in Wellington, New Zealand, he went to Leipzig where he played violin in the Gewandhaus Orchestra under Brahms, Dvo ák and Bruch, and returning to this region spent his long life teaching and composing in both of his 'native' countries. He was a prime mover in the establishment of the NSW (later Sydney) Conservatorium; his compositions include twelve symphonies, eight operas, seventeen string quartets and numerous small works. His style, as might be expected, is a genially late-Romantic one; Covell has rightly noted that Hill doesn't quite cut it as a 'grand old man'. His works are always well crafted and coherent if often lacking in strong personality, and it might be said that the stylistic manners of Brahms, Dvoák and Bruch lingered in Hill's work long after they had been overtaken elsewhere.

Hill believed passionately in the need to raise antipodean musical consciousness. Some of his works try, perhaps too hard, to be 'national' while remaining firmly middle-European in manner. On the other hand, Hill very early became interested in the indigenous music of Australia, New Zealand and New Guinea. While one of his most famous pieces, *Waiata Poi*, teeters on the brink of kitsch, there is a touching story of Hill singing a traditional chant to a Maori chambermaid in an Auckland hotel: 'You sing better than my father' was her response.[3] Like his British and European contemporaries, Hill could see that indigenous music was endangered, and encouraged the collection of such music in New Zealand. In 1950, he enthused to the *Sydney Morning Herald* about a huge number of recordings made in Central and Northern Australia:

> There is enough material in these recordings to start an entirely Australian school of music, as different in idiom as Vaughan Williams and the English school from anything else. It's a gold mine. If I had had anything like that in New Zealand 50 years ago; but it was too late.[4]

Aboriginal melodies had been notated as early as the beginning of the nineteenth century and several tunes had found their way into published form 'arranged' by composers. Hill's wife Mirrie (1892–1986), a fine composer in her own right, wrote in the 1950s a number of works using Aboriginal melodies collected by the anthropologist CP Mountford, as well as her Symphony in A, *Arnhem Land*. But one gets the sense of a lost opportunity which was in some respects recaptured in the 1960s, though by then the depredation of Aboriginal culture in much of Australia was sadly complete. It goes without saying that in those areas of the country which were readily converted to farm-land, especially in the south-eastern states, Aboriginal communities were 'dispersed' or perished as a result of western disease much earlier. Those cultures which have survived have tended to do so in country which is inimical to European farming practices, such as the deserts of Central Australia, and there, paradoxically, the western disciplines of anthropology and linguistics have helped to conserve or rebuild indigenous cultures.

One of Australia's most celebrated musical eccentrics, Percy Grainger (1882–1961)[5], was a major figure alongside Vaughan Williams and Holst in the collection of British and Scandinavian folk music, but as a permanent expatriate he didn't get much time to look into indigenous music, though he did hear music from the Central Australian Aranda people recorded on wax cylinders by anthropologists Baldwin Spencer and Francis Gillen. He did write a piece called *The lonely desert man sees the huts of his tribe*, and in one of his most enduring works, *The Warriors*, he writes an imaginary ballet of warrior tribes from all over the world. But in 1946, the composer John Antill (1904–1986) made a splash when Eugene Goossens conducted movements from his ballet, *Corroboree*, which evoked certain Aboriginal myths and rituals. Antill's piece is, and could only ever be, a synthetic and inauthentic western artefact, which is by no means to suggest that it was bad music – far from it. But it does signal a growing interest in making Australian music into something distinct.

In some respects the Australian music scene of the 1960s resembles nothing so much as that of Russia a century before. There are several parallels between two countries modernising culturally and technologically, at great speed, whose populations were aware of the potentially swamping effect of the more established institutions of Europe. We shouldn't forget that Tchaikovsky was in the first graduating class from the St Petersburg Conservatorium, and that his colleagues such as 'The Five' (Balakirev, Borodin, Cui, Mussorgsky and Rimsky-Korsakov) were adamantly opposed, at first, to the importation of European techniques and forms. To push the Russian metaphor just a little further, we might say that Peter Sculthorpe is Australia's Balakirev, with the British musicologist Wilfred Mellers as VI Stasov, the influential journalist who boosted the whole idea of a national Russian music. Mellers encouraged Sculthorpe to think along national lines, and, as Professor of Music at the University of York, was mentor to a number of younger Australians. In some respects Australia was having the sorts of cultural conversations which had already been had and resolved elsewhere decades if not centuries earlier. The composers who emerged in the 1960s raised a number of questions about the nature of Australian music – a conversation we had to have to sort out our real or imagined relationships to Europe, to Aboriginal Australia and to our geographic region. As we will see, some of those conversations, notably about the ethics and aesthetics of blending western and traditional Aboriginal music, are ongoing, but in general a national idiom is no longer a pressing issue. Thanks to many of the composers we're discussing, we can now have the confidence to look outwards and become part of the international musical community.

Not, of course, that there haven't been Australian composers of international stature and confident mien. Percy Grainger, for one, enjoyed pop-star status as a young pianist-composer while dreaming of what he called 'free music' – free from the restrictions of the western scale – and invented machines for playing it. Melbourne-born Peggy Glanville-Hicks divided her time as composer and critic between Europe and the United States. Arthur Benjamin (1893–1960) spent his working life in Britain from the 1920s on (being an important teacher of the young Benjamin Britten) as did the more recent Malcolm Williamson (1931–2003), a former protégé of Britten's who rose to become Master of the Queen's Music.

So, while some of these figures left Australia on a more or less permanent basis, the different waves of migration to Australia inevitably influenced composition here. There were the British, Scots and Irish, and the Chinese during the gold rushes. During the first third of the twentieth century Melbourne became the third largest Greek city after Athens and Thessalonica. We gladly took in refugees from the so-called 'captive nations' of the Baltic. Large communities of Turkish and Lebanese people established themselves here. There was also a scheme in the 1960s whereby people from the UK could come to Australia for ten pounds if they agreed to settle here. And in the 1970s Malcolm Fraser, an otherwise conservative prime minister, decided that as we had helped bomb the citizens of Vietnam, the only decent thing was to overturn the White Australia Policy and offer homes to Indo-Chinese refugees. As the new century wears on, the countries from which people migrate become even more diverse.

Importantly for this discussion, there was a large influx of middle-European migrants after World War II, among them a number of Hungarians, Germans and Austrians – many Jewish – who brought with them an expectation of the kind of musical life that they had enjoyed before the war. Those communities produced a number of composers who baffled local audiences with what they regarded as 'way out' music. Other members of those communities founded Musica Viva Australia, which has subsequently become a unique entrepreneur of chamber music, importing the finest ensembles for national tours, supporting the best local artists and running education programs throughout Australia and Singapore. Musica Viva has an honourable history of commissioning new works: shortly after Alfred Hill's death, Mirrie Hill gave the organisation money to establish a commission in his memory, and the first work that emerged was Sculthorpe's String Quartet No. 6. It was followed in 1966 by the seventh quartet, which he later renamed *Red Landscape*, an indication of the composer's ongoing interest in imaging aspects of Australia's landscape in his work. In this he was not alone, as we'll see in the next sections.

Chapter 3

'The' Australian Landscape

... and yonder all before us lye
Desarts of vast Eternity.

'To his coy mistress', Andrew Marvell (1621–78)

The Melbourne composer Henry Tate (1873–1926) had advocated bird-song as the basis for a national music in a series of articles published just before his death. Sadly, Tate didn't live to see just how prophetic he proved to be: Sculthorpe has provided musical images of birdsong in countless pieces and a work like *Mandala V* by David Lumsdaine (born 1931), resident in the UK since 1953, is full of the precisely rendered sounds of Australian birds. Lumsdaine and his colleague Moya Henderson (born 1941) have both, incidentally, composed radiophonic works using the recorded sound of Australian birds.

Lumsdaine's *Cambewarra Mountain* is a large-scale work in which the patterns of recorded birdcalls are treated like themes in a symphonic piece; Henderson takes a quite different approach in *Currawong*, using 'the bolshy feeding noises and the crashlandings on tin sheds by scrub turkeys'.[1] Ron Nagorcka (born 1948), late of Melbourne but now to be found in the Tasmanian bush, also makes much use of recorded birdsong. Finally, to overcome a crisis of style and meaning in the 1970s, Ross Edwards (born 1943) found himself listening intently to the insect sounds of the Sydney basin. The distinctive shapes, timing and phasing of such sounds have been a crucial part of the development of his personal style. These are unique sounds to Australia, but here the composer has assimilated them for their abstract value.

All these are attempts to use the ambient sounds of this country to create a distinctive music, and no composer has been more preoccupied with the notion of Australian music than Peter Sculthorpe. Sculthorpe was born in Tasmania in 1929 and studied at the University of Melbourne's Conservatorium from 1946 where he received great encouragement from the then Ormond Professor, Bernard Heinze, while studying with JA Steele. In his biography of Sculthorpe, Graeme Skinner notes that Heinze regarded these years as the Conservatorium's 'Golden age': in the aftermath of World War II the institution found itself full of ex-service personnel and young musicians of European background. Sculthorpe's direct contemporaries, in and outside the 'Con', included George Dreyfus (born 1928) and Felix Werder (born 1922) to whose work we'll return. The latter, as Skinner notes, introduced Sculthorpe to the ideas and practice of Schoenberg, though atonality and serialism were not to leave a lasting impression on Sculthorpe's music. After Melbourne, Sculthorpe travelled to the UK for study at Wadham College, Oxford, but returned to Australia in 1960 owing to the serious illness of his father. The latter died in 1961 and Sculthorpe's memorial to him was *Irkanda IV* for violin, percussion and strings. By his own estimation it is Sculthorpe's first mature work; its Aboriginal title, evocation of space and profound melancholy are all elements that are central to his output.

For Sculthorpe, the term 'distinctly Australian' equated in some way with the evocation of a unique geography. There are, of course, many different landscapes in Australia but the image of a vast, flat, desert (which indeed much of the interior is) has been translated in certain works into a music characterised by a slow rate of change, a tendency to use drone basses as emblematic of the eternal quality of the desert and, against this background, busier, local events – the evocation of birdsong and the like. Notwithstanding his great friendship with the painter Russell Drysdale, many of Sculthorpe's 'landscape' pieces thus have their visual analogue more in the work of Fred Williams who, like the composer, had a particular understanding of background stasis and foreground detail. These musical concerns are particularly evident in works like *Sun Music I* where colourful, fragmentary events take place against static drones or luminous clouds of sound. Sculthorpe was not, of course, the first or only composer to image distinctively Australian ambient sound, and as we've noted, this was not an idea that appeared magically in the 1960s.

Sculthorpe interpreted the term *irkanda* in a series of works as a 'lonely place', and in much of his landscape music the canvas is one devoid of human figures. Other composers, like Australian painters and writers, have seen the outback landscapes as a locus of the struggle between nature and culture – a struggle which, given the harshness of such landscapes, takes on a particular urgency for the European trying to survive. It has therefore provided a powerful backdrop for works such as the music-theatre piece *Edward John Eyre* (1973) by Barry Conyngham. One of the first generation of Sculthorpe's students, Conyngham's interest in landscape has two main expressions: he contemplates specific kinds of landscapes (in abstract pieces like the concertos *Monuments*, *Waterways* and *Cloudlines*) in order to create what he calls 'an inner personal world ... a magic place to go, a place where beauty and completeness is all there is'[2]; by contrast, landscape can create the stage where he depicts the effects of isolation on the human self. *Edward John Eyre* dramatises Eyre's near-disastrous cross-country expedition across the Nullarbor from Adelaide to King George Sound on the southern coast of Western Australia in 1840–41. It is instructive of the different ways in which Indigenous and white Australians saw themselves both in the landscape and in relation to each other. Eyre is also the central figure in David Lumsdaine's *Aria for Edward John Eyre* of 1972. This work, for two narrators, soprano, ensemble and tape, was commissioned by British soprano Jane Manning, bassist Barry Guy and the London Sinfonietta and effectively creates a sense of hallucinatory isolation in its use of spacious harmonies, in the alienating effect of two narrators reading together but out of time, and in the disjunct writing for soprano and the refraction of her voice into many by tape-delay.

In 1986 *Voss* by Richard Meale finally took to the stage at the Adelaide Festival. The opera, with libretto by David Malouf, was based on the novel by Patrick White which in turn is a fictionalised account of the career of explorer Ludwig Leichhardt. (Leichhardt rather embarrassingly arrived back in Sydney as its denizens were mourning his untimely death with a cantata by Isaac Nathan (1790–1864). Nathan has the distinction of being Australia's first professional composer and, having been killed by a horse-drawn tram, one its first road fatalities. Leichhardt's second expedition did, however, end badly.) *Voss* is an epic tragedy of a German explorer and his doomed party, and a kind of mystically telepathic relationship between Voss and Laura Trevelyan, the step-daughter of one of his financial backers in Sydney.

Like *Voss*, Moya Henderson's *Lindy* (to a libretto by Judith Rodriguez) was years in the making, and like it deals with a tragic death in the wilderness. In this case the death was that of baby Azaria Chamberlain and the miscarriage of justice which saw her mother, Lindy, excoriated in the press and public opinion and wrongfully imprisoned. *Lindy*'s long-delayed stage premiere in 2002 came about only after protracted and unedifying brawling between composer and conductor; the trimmed-down result is perhaps not what the composer had in mind but was arguably less unwieldy on stage. More recently, a collaboration between composer Andrew Schultz (born 1960) and writer Gordon Kalton Williams saw the creation of *Journey to Horseshoe Bend*,

Death scene from the Australian Opera's 1990 production of *Voss* by
Richard Meale and David Malouf, directed by Jim Sharman, rehearsed by
Brian Fitzgerald and designed by Brian Thomson (sets), Luciana Arrighi
(costumes), Nigel Levings (lighting) and choreography by Chrissie Koltai.
Eilene Hannan as Laura, Alan Dargin as Jacky, Geoffrey Chard as Voss.
Photo by Branco Gaica.

a symphonic cantata dramatising a traumatic incident in the life of the young TGH Strehlow (later to become an important and contentious figure in Australian anthropology and Aboriginal studies).

All of these works pose the question of how to depict the Australian desert in music, both as a backdrop for the drama of humanity in an extreme state and as a character in itself. We've seen that in a number of cases Sculthorpe has 'translated' the character of the outback into music with static background and intermittently busy foreground, a kind of visual analogue in sound. Curiously, none of the composers mentioned here — Meale, Conyngham, Henderson, Lumsdaine or Schultz — make use of those techniques.

Opera in the Outback:
Voss, Lindy and *Journey to Horseshoe Bend*

Patrick White's 1957 novel *Voss* was an attempt to write in a mode far removed from 'the dreary, dun-coloured offspring of journalistic realism'.[3] The story of his fictional explorer is a metaphysical and visionary one; the essentially solitary Voss is clearly a mythical and, in the final analysis, a messianic hero and the Australian landscape the setting for the kind of spiritual revelation experienced by biblical prophets and Christ himself. The story White tells is extremely simple: the German explorer who claims the country 'by right of vision' leaves colonial Sydney to travel into the interior with a group of white settlers and Aboriginal guides. Sydney society is portrayed as stifling and provincial, peopled by settlers who think Voss and his expedition mad. Only Laura Trevelyan, the niece of one of his financial backers, recognises Voss' true nature. While she remains in Sydney, the story elaborates their spiritual affinity. Voss' party is eventually beaten by the landscape and internal politics; all while characters die, with Voss himself being beheaded by one of the Aboriginal guides. The inevitable nature of this is summed up in Voss' remark in Act II: 'The mystery of life is not solved by my success, but failure, by perpetual struggle, in becoming.'[4]

Meale's librettist for the opera was the distinguished poet and novelist David Malouf, and together they produced a scenario of two acts. The first takes place in Sydney, establishing the nature of colonial society and the relationships among the principal characters. (It is here that Meale makes amusing use of those quadrilles, *La Illawarra* and so on, mentioned earlier.) The second act takes place, often simultaneously, in both Sydney and in the outback, stressing the mystical communion between Voss and Laura. Largely for that reason, the music seldom attempts simple scene painting, concentrating instead on the psychology of the characters. The landscape itself is in a sense depicted by its musical absence. In Act II scene 2, for instance, there is one of the many mystical duets in this work. Here Voss conjures the desert: 'Our shadows lead us deeper into ourselves, into the redness of fire, the inferno of love, into the sun'. It is clearly a metaphorical desert, and the music in which it is cast is mythological, with heaving Wagnerian figures in the orchestral bass and gnawing repeated chords. As the duet progresses into frankly gorgeous music the models are as much Puccini and the Bartók of *Bluebeard's Castle* as anyone. When the pious Palfreyman begins his Christmas hymn, the bells and brass take us into the sound world of Britten's *Peter Grimes*, while Voss sleepwalks to Ravel-like woodwind arabesques. Le Mesurier sings an aria of how he will shortly die and become one with the land, just before he is speared by the Aborigines; the music here has hints, as Roger Covell has remarked in his notes to the recording of this work, of the 'Aboriginal' sounds of Antill's *Corroboree*. None of which is a criticism: Meale's music shows just how the characters are constructed by their European-ness, and how that is a factor in their destruction. For Voss, civilisation is a barrier between the self and the infinite.

Moya Henderson has justifiably referred to *Lindy* as a 'white woman's dreaming'. Lindy Chamberlain was accused and convicted of the murder of her baby daughter Azaria at Uluru (Ayer's Rock) in 1980. Chamberlain's defence was that one of the dingos that lived in the area had taken her baby from the tent in which they were camping. She was eventually pardoned and her defence accepted when the bloodied jacket of a small child was found at the site, dramatically vindicating her version of events. The story has many of the elements of opera and myth, especially the infanticidal mother and the individual ostracised and hounded by society. As mentioned earlier, when *Lindy* finally took to the stage it was in a version considerably shorter than the composer's original, though it is quite possible that the cuts imposed made for a more easily staged work. Be that as it may, these elements remained intact, although the truncation sadly meant the omission of the Aboriginal trackers as singing characters.

Much of the work as it finally appeared takes place in environments where Chamberlain's persecution can be dramatised: in prison and courtroom. A crucial scene is that in which Azaria disappears as her parents socialise with other visitors to Uluru. Bearing in mind Henderson's radiophonic work *Currawong*, it is unsurprising that birdsong features at this point in the opera, where the natural environment comes to the fore: the call of the butcherbird singing at night provides the talking point for the Chamberlains and another couple. Its song is rendered in the sound of flutes and punctuates the scene of easy friendliness and admiration for the desert sky which is shattered by the realisation that Azaria has been taken.

In *Voss* and *Lindy* the outback landscape is the locus or setting for epic struggle − in Voss' case the painful dissolution of the socially constructed ego symbolised by beheading (which, we should stress, is symbolic, not a representation of common Aboriginal practice); in that of Lindy Chamberlain, the scene of the death that precipitates her tragedy. While the symphonic cantata *Journey to Horseshoe Bend* is not an opera, it is nonetheless dramatic in impact like the Bach Cantatas and Passions from which it ultimately descends. (Incidentally, the US director Peter Sellars has enjoyed some success in staging Bach's cantatas.) This work, composed by Andrew Schultz to a libretto by Gordon Kalton Williams, is based on the autobiographical novel of the same name by TGH (Ted) Strehlow (1908−1978). Strehlow's father was the Lutheran missionary at Hermannsburg, about 120 kilometres west-southwest of Alice Springs. Ted Strehlow was born there and grew up speaking Aranda (or Arrernte) as well as German and English. In later life he would return to Central Australia in various capacities, and there would record and film traditional Aranda song and ceremony (at the Aranda people's request) and take sacred objects into his protection. In 1922 his father Carl Strehlow became gravely ill and needed to be taken, by horse-drawn vehicle, to the rail head at Oodnadatta for a train to Adelaide. The journey was arduous and extremely painful for the suffering pastor, who died at Horseshoe Bend on the Finke River. In his novel, Strehlow recounts the events: leaving Hermannsburg, the testing of the sick man's faith in such suffering and the growing sense in the young boy of his own identity with that landscape and its people. Schultz's score calls for solo boy soprano, representing young Ted Strehlow, solo bass baritone for his father, two narrators, the Ntarea Ladies Choir from Hermannsburg, and four-part chorus.[5] The large orchestra is physically divided into a central 'river valley' group, two 'ridges' and, across the back and sides of the stage, a group of percussionist representing 'distant sites', allowing a range of terrific spatial effects and a variety of textures which are never dense.

Schultz, like Meale and Henderson, avoids the trap of depicting the desert as featureless and 'other' in his music, and Williams' libretto is richly endowed with Indigenous creation stories that bring alive the landscape in 'Aboriginal' terms. Moreover, the Strehlows felt at home in Central Australia; rather than evoke a hostile and alien landscape, this work makes clear that the departure is unwilled and in some degree traumatic for all concerned. Each of the cantata's three sections is associated with a particular place on the journey, beginning in Hermannsburg where the Aboriginal congregation is heard at first talking about this man they so respect and then singing, in Carl Strehlow's Aranda translation, the Lutheran chorale 'Wachet auf!'. The central section 'Idracowra' is the 'Act II' of a classical drama, where Carl experiences the darkness of doubt, while in the final section, 'Horseshoe Bend', Carl dies. In dramatic counterpoint to this story is that of the landscape itself and the ancestral beings that created and

I am a white boy,   I am my fath-er's son   I play with your sons

Andrew Schultz/Gordon Kalton Williams: *Journey to Horseshoe Bend*, bars 102–07 showing the use of Phrygian mode intervals. Used by permission of the composer.

sustain it. Among these, the 'Rain women' make a dramatic intervention after Carl's death as the storm, which has been gathering for the preceding days, breaks. The symbolism of life in death is powerful and provides the composer with an occasion for shattering music.

Schultz's musical language in this work is wide ranging. He never directly quotes Aboriginal traditional music – there is in fact no dramatically compelling reason to have done so. He does give the boy Ted a melodic character that stresses Phrygian intervals, notably a falling semitone-major third-whole tone pattern, evoking sounds that we hear in much Aboriginal and Asian-inflected Australian music to underline his affinity with the land (see music example). The chorales (some by, or associated with, JS Bach, and two by Schultz himself) act, as in a traditional cantata, as structural pivots, and provide motivic fragments and other melodic material that is threaded through the work. And there is Schultz's own style based on a lucid, essentially diatonic harmony, an ability to write long-spanned melodies and a fine ear for orchestration.

It is the orchestration of this work in particular in which Schultz addresses the issue of representing the landscape. Some of the material from the first section is derived from a chamber work called *Tonic Continent* whose opening gesture is textbook landscape music with a drone supporting simple melodies characterised by repeated notes in even quavers. But more importantly, *Journey to Horseshoe Bend* uses that gesture as a starting point, preferring more inventive solutions to the depiction of light and space. And rather than creating a musical analogue in two dimensions – drone and foreground – Schultz's spatial deployment of the orchestra becomes a kind of hologram of this fascinating place.

Chapter 4

Going Native?

Significantly, in recent years Peter Sculthorpe has re-examined a number of earlier works to find that the timbre of the didjeridu melds effortlessly with his scoring. Several more recent compositions, ranging from string quartets to his choral-orchestral Requiem of 2004 (not to be confused with the 1979 Requiem for cello alone), include a didjeridu as integral to the instrumentation. This of course relates to another aspect of Sculthorpe's sense of the spirit of place: the allusion to, or even direct quotation of, music of Indigenous Australians. As we've seen, composers like Grainger and Antill evoked a real or imagined Aboriginal work in certain pieces but without the use of actual Aboriginal material. Sculthorpe's *The Song of Tailitnama*, a setting of Aranda verse collected (and translated) by TGH Strehlow, uses a melody not unrelated to a Groote Eylandt song; the work appears in a number of versions, vocal and instrumental, and forms a significant element in such works as *Earth Cry* for orchestra. Sculthorpe has used some of the earliest notations of Aboriginal music in a number of works; in the 2004 Requiem the 'Maranoa Lullaby', collected in Queensland in the 1930s and published by Allan's, contrasts and melds with Gregorian chant and with Sculthorpe's own late style.

This opens the delicate issue of appropriation. For a composer like Bartók or Vaughan Williams to use folk song as the basis for art music continues a process of osmosis which has been happening in European music since notation was invented, but Aboriginal music has, for the overwhelming majority of white Australians, always been 'other'. Fortunately, as white Australia has become increasingly aware of Aboriginal cultural sensitivities, we have come to understand that culture's intricate relationship of songs, dances and ancestral stories, physical sites and ritual objects which are owned by specific individuals and which are taboo to others. Accordingly it can be seen as discourteous, to say the very least, for non-Indigenous artists to appropriate material which may be sacred, and they must understand the need to ask permission and respect any restriction imposed by the owners of the material. In the case of music, however, it does point up a fundamental difference between Aboriginal and western perspectives: in the former, the sacred – be it chant, story or object – is inextricably involved with the secret; a Gregorian chant, by contrast, will often be linked to a specific liturgical time or season but is nonetheless available to all.

There are thus serious ethical issues involved in the use of actual Aboriginal material. Works by more recent non-Indigenous composers circumvent these issues to some extent by producing 'synthetic' versions of Aboriginal music from distinctive elements: the short-long rhythmic patterns of clap-sticks, melodies which begin high in the vocal register and follow a downwards trajectory through 'gapped' scale passages, the universally recognised sounds of the didjeridu. Using the didjeridu as a cipher of Australianness is common, though it should be noted that the instrument is historically restricted to the wet tropics of northern Australia. One of the most striking early attempts to blend the didjeridu with western instruments was George Dreyfus' Sextet for Wind quintet and didjeridu of 1971 which, in effect, exploited the huge technological gulf between the didjeridu and modern instruments: the didjeridu is notated as a single dark line in the score, against which the other instruments play often extravagantly virtuosic music. Dreyfus is one of that generation of German Jewish refugees whose openness to the ideas of the post-war European avant-garde was such an important element in the changes to Australian music in the 1960s. He again used the didjeridu in his music theatre work, *Rathenau*, the story of the Jewish Foreign Minister in the Weimar Republic, murdered by extremists in the rise of Nazism. In both cases, of course, the instrument is used not for any connotative function but for its timbral possibilities.

The temptation to treat the didjeridu as a drone is great, and as ethnomusicologist Stephen Knopoff[1] has pointed out, that is its most common use in western Arnhem Land. But elsewhere its musical function is much more varied and complex. In 1974 Roger Smalley (born 1943), a British-born composer who had studied with, among others, Karlheinz Stockhausen, came to Perth for what was to be a short residency. Smalley's first 'Australian' composition was an electronic piece based on a recording of a piece for didjeridu from Mornington Island: not long after he had arrived in Australia, Smalley had encountered the sound of the didjeridu and 'was struck by its extraordinary rhythmic complexity and by several similarities to electronic techniques (e.g. the filtering of an overtone spectrum, modulation of the tone by the player's voice)'.[2] In other words, the didjeridu player produces a huge variety of sounds, some of which are clearly imitative of natural noises, others the product of sophisticated modifications of sound production. Like Smalley, composers who have subsequently written for the didjeridu have exploited the techniques that he describes.

The often-overlooked Margaret Sutherland composed her only opera *The Young Kabbarli* on a story from the life of the intrepid Daisy Bates who lived with and wrote about Aboriginal communities in Western and South Australia. The opera, with a libretto by Maie Casey, was premiered, somewhat surprisingly, in Hobart in 1965. It must be one of the first works for the operatic stage which includes the sound of the didjeridu, although we should note Sutherland's use of the instru-ment is anomalous in that it is not native to the regions depicted in the opera but rather is a cipher or symbol for Aboriginality. Colin Bright's *Earth Spirit* (1989), however, lays claim to be 'the first composition for the Western symphony orchestra featuring didjeridus ... It explores sounds both in-common and not, with the orchestra eventually becom-ing a giant didjeridu'.[3] Bright (born 1949), who is based in Sydney, is a composer with a burning sense of social justice and faith in art's power to proclaim political values. He has worked with students in disad-vantaged schools, raised money for Aboriginal land rights through his music, and much of his work engages directly with important political issues. With some justification, Bright claimed a socio-political victory in having two didjeridus – one played by the composer and the other by an Indigenous performer, Kevin Duncan – on stage with the Sydney Symphony Orchestra for *Earth Spirit*. Two decades later the charis-matic didjeridu virtuoso William Barton is a frequent star performer on concert platforms around the world (though a standing ovation at the Sydney Opera House in early 2008 didn't stop him being refused entry to a pretentious Sydney noshery later that night. He's Aboriginal, you see.)

David Tacey, an associate professor of English at Melbourne's La Trobe University, has explored the notion of Australian spirituality in a number of books, notably *Edge of the Sacred* (1995). In that book he makes the claim that 'in Australia, where land and Aboriginality are fused ... white Australians, virtually in spite of themselves are becom-ing slowly Aboriginalised in the subconscious'.[4] Tacey doesn't mean that the general population's average life expectancy is plummeting by decades and its infant mortality rate rising, that it will have unac-ceptable levels of preventable disease or welfare dependency, that a disproportionate number of its citizens are in gaol at any given time or will be barred entrance to Sydney nightspots. He's talking about the *subconscious*, so no-one gets hurt; his notion has been leapt upon and much quoted by Australian composers and musicologists. It is largely a Romantic fantasy, especially in the light of patterns of consumption

Didjeridu virtuoso and composer William Barton. Photo by Bridget Elliot.

in early twenty-first century Australia. (Richard Taruskin in his recent *Oxford History of Western Music* takes the fans of the Holy Minimalists – Gorecki, Taverner, Pärt – to task for wanting 'to return "Aesthetically" or "appreciatively" to a world of "spiritual wholeness" without assuming the burdens of actual religious commitment'.[5] One could make the same criticism of certain white Australians who fantasise about 'becoming Aboriginal' in the safety of middle-class suburbia.)

However, whether it counts as 'Aboriginalisation', the way in which non-Indigenous composers approach Aboriginal music is now much less imperialist and more collegiate; where once 'Aboriginal melodies' were simply imported into 'classical' music, the last two decades have seen a much more dialogic approach. Non-Indigenous composers have increasingly collaborated with Aboriginal musicians, in part to express political solidarity with a severely disadvantaged group of fellow citizens and in part to enrich the potential of musical language. And not just the musical language of the concert hall or opera theatre; Aboriginal culture is as changeable and dynamic as any other, and these collaborations have the potential to enrich it as well.

Barton (born 1981) has himself been the catalyst for several substantial new works by composers with whom he has collaborated. He has worked with Brisbane-based composer Sean O'Boyle (born 1963) on a concerto that devotes its four movements to each of the elements of earth, wind, water and fire. Much of the musical material was collaboratively devised, though the tendency towards big tunes and technicolour scoring can be put down to O'Boyle's extensive experience of composition for the screen. More recently Barton, in addition to his own composing, has worked with Elena Kats-Chernin (born 1957) on *The C* for piano and didjeridu (2007) and a new collaborative concerto with Matthew Hindson (born 1968), *Kalkadungu*. Full of sound and fury, this work is based on a chant written by Barton at the age of 15. It reflects on his ancestral Kalkadunga people (from the area of present-day Mount Isa), especially their resistance to and ultimate defeat by the forces of white colonisation. The creative process behind *Kalkadungu* is therefore similar to that behind Liza Lim's *The Compass*, the most successful work for didjeridu and western instruments so far. Interestingly, Lim (born 1966) speculated (in Andrew Ford's 2001 *Dots on the Landscape* radio series[6]) on a scenario whereby orchestral musicians might live on the traditional lands of the didjeridu player before collaborating in performance. This didn't happen with *The Compass*, though Perth-based composer Iain Grandage (born 1970) did manage to have members of the West Australian Symphony Orchestra spend time with the Spinifex people in south-eastern Western Australia in preparation for his (as yet unperformed) *Ooldea*.

There is, needless to say, plenty of music that refers to Aboriginal history, cosmology or spirituality without necessarily including traditional instruments or material. One of the most significant of such pieces was written by the visiting English composer Michael Finnissy: his *Banumbirr* (1982) for flute, clarinet, violin, cello and piano was, he explains, 'inspired by an Aboriginal Australian bark-painting of Banumbirr, the morning star. Beyond trying to find – empathically – musical "gestures" within myself that corresponded to the hieratic (totemic/symbolic) patterns and deliberately restricted colours of that painting, there are no other connections with the indigenous art of Australia.'[7] Finnissy isn't alone among foreign composers: his compatriot Peter Maxwell Davies has likewise found inspiration in Aboriginal 'dreaming' stories as has Tōru Takemitsu. Back home, Moya Henderson's string quartet *Kudikynah Cave* (1987) celebrates an important cultural site in Tasmania, while her piano trio, *Waking up the flies* (1990) refers to a colloquialism among Aboriginal women who comfort a mourner by stroking her back, thus 'waking up the flies'. In both cases Henderson's musical style is unequivocally western, using an essentially modal harmony and conventional deployment of instruments; in *Sacred Site* for organ, Henderson turns this on its head, celebrating the site of the Sydney Opera House which was previously a tram depot and before that, of course, part of the lands of the original inhabitants. The Luxembourg-born but Sydney resident Georges Lentz (born 1965) has been engaged for many years on an ongoing cycle of works called *Mysterium* which explores the classical idea of the Music of the Spheres. This collection of pieces, in which Lentz moves effortlessly from the simplest diatonic sound to extraordinarily imagined advanced textures, from solo prepared piano to full orchestral score, contains works whose titles allude to Aboriginal cosmology and spirituality and several of these use words for stars in a variety of Aboriginal languages: *Guyuhmgan, Ngangkar, Monh*. Lentz has explained, too, that his feeling for Aboriginal spirituality is mediated by the immensely complex designs in dot painting by artists like Kathleen Petyarre and the late Emily Kame Kngwarreye. Another Sydney-based composer, Paul Stanhope (born 1969), has likewise been fascinated by Aboriginal mythology and cosmology; he has also set poetry by the late Oodgeroo Noonuccal (formerly Kath Walker), *Songs for the Shadowland*, which movingly depicts aspects of twentieth-century Indigenous life.

Those composers who began to explore Aboriginal and Asian music and aesthetics in the 1960s and 1970s were all ethnically European and were self-consciously exploring beyond the porous edges of western culture. Similar things were happening in the music of European and American composers at the time; here, owing to our geographical proximity to Asia and to the unique nature of our landscapes, our composers felt they were exploring something distinctly and newly Australian. At their best they succeeded, but occasionally the experiment failed, with works of unarguable sincerity still sounding like travelogue soundtracks. In the work of Liza Lim, whose career began in the late 1980s, these disparate elements are inevitably more integrated.

Liza Lim and the Branching Song

Lim's earliest works include several written for mixed ensemble – she has had an ongoing relationship with the Elision Ensemble since its foundation, and has been commissioned by numerous other new music ensembles here and in Europe. Her ensemble music is highly gestural with an ear for subtle and intense colour and the dramatic use of sudden quietness, if not silence, and she has gone beyond traditional western instruments to compose idiomatically for the Japanese *koto* and Chinese *qin*.

Lim's orchestral work begins with *Cathedral* (1994) in which she characteristically explores the idea of resonance in space, a concern equally evident in *Ecstatic Architecture*, commissioned by the Los Angeles Philharmonic for its inaugural season in the Frank Gehry-designed Walt Disney Concert Hall a decade later. A period as composer-in-residence with the Sydney Symphony Orchestra produced three works. *Immer fliessender* (2004) is a kind of prelude to Mahler's Ninth Symphony in which Lim magically distils whole swathes of Mahlerian sound into single gestures, while *Flying Banner (After Wang To)* (2005) plays with the standard gambits of fanfares before dissolving into the cross-hatching patterns of cicada calls. The most substantial outcome of the residency was *The Compass*, one of several new Australian pieces that feature the considerable talents of didjeridu soloist William Barton.

Lim is well aware of the essential difference between writing for ensemble – however large – and an orchestra, describing the challenge of 'how to activate a large mass of sound without losing the detailing of colour and gestural nuance that has been so central to my musical language'. The specific challenge in *The Compass* is how to manage 'the "torque" (like driving a car) of how different instrumental groupings respond and sound ... where solo lines and massed groups move in counterpoint at different rates'.[8] Lim's deployment of the orchestra in *The Compass* is, strange as it may seem, comparable to that of Bruckner in his symphonies. Lim's 'massed groups' are very often instrumental families moving at different speeds: typically, woodwind groups often have the fastest moving passagework; shimmering fabrics of sound are spun out of rapid, high string ostinatos; there are two instances of a chorale-like passage for brass that moves at a stately pace through an otherwise febrile texture. Of course, *The Compass* sounds nothing like Bruckner, though for both composers music is a means of celebrating the transcendental.

The Compass is unique in the way in which it combines and synthesises western and Indigenous traditions. The two didjeridus required

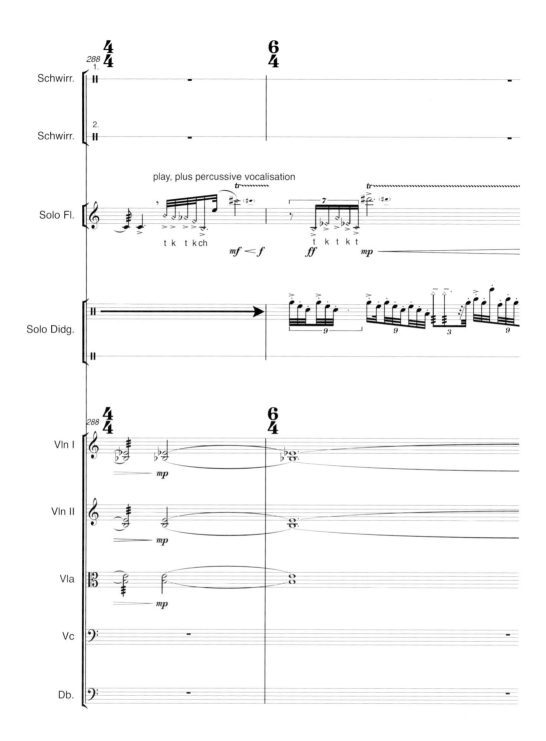

Liza Lim: *The Compass*, page 60. Note the extreme virtuosic writing for both flute and didjeridu soloists. Used by permission of Universal Music.

(with fundamental pitches of A and C) 'provide a bass line, but also generate the fundamental sonorities which resonate throughout the orchestra'. In what western music calls 'equal temperament', the chromatic scale is divided by equal semitones into twelve notes. In the natural harmonic series, however, as we get higher and further away from the fundamental or lowest pitch, the overtones get closer together and sound 'out of tune' to ears used only to equal temperament. What Lim does in this work is to use those microtonal differences as the basis for the work's harmony. All the instruments in the orchestra for *The Compass* (apart from the piano) can produce microtones: woodwinds can 'bend' notes using embouchure (the position of the mouth) or cross-fingering or can over-blow to produce 'out-of-tune' upper partials; brass can play 'natural' harmonics rather than using the valves which enable them to play in equal temperament; string players can move their fingers fractionally away from 'in tune' notes on the fingerboard. So there are galvanising moments when the didjeridu uses the full gamut of vocalisations, overtones, howls and wails which are taken up by the whole orchestra.

The solo flautist plays three instruments in *The Compass*: the concert flute in C, piccolo and amplified bass flute. Lim's writing for the flute family makes use of the research by Carin Levine into extended techniques, particularly multiphonics – chords produced by a combination of cross-fingering and overblowing. (Levine was flute soloist in the European premiere of *The Compass*; Rosamund Plummer gave the world premiere with the Sydney Symphony Orchestra in 2006.) Other extended techniques include vocalising – singing, whispering and growling through the instrument – techniques obviously related to those of the didjeridu.

The Compass avoids any simplistic opposition such as ancient didjeridu versus modern hi-tech flute. In fact Lim is well aware that, being a wooden artefact native to wet-tropical northern Australia, the didjeridu's archaeological record is not extensive, where the flute is demonstrably one of the oldest creations of human technology. Lim also avoids using the didjeridu (and Barton) as a Romantic cipher for an imagined, static, pre-lapsarian culture. It is a *synthetic* work in two senses of the word (neither pejorative): it brings together and unites two different musical traditions, and it is a work which recognises the constantly changing aspect of any culture. For instance, the words of the unaccompanied chant sung at the work's opening were composed by Barton and Lim. They are in his ancestral Kalkadoon language, but translated by Barton from English with the aid of a dictionary. The chant has many of the hallmarks of traditional Aboriginal melody, in that it begins high in the singer's range, contains patterns of repeated notes and, overall, moves downwards by step. But, as Lim notes, it 'makes no claims to being "authentic" in any narrow sense ... But that is part of the point of the work: the cultural backgrounds of both composer and performer are dynamic and adaptable.'

In English the text of the chant reads: 'The Heart Sits in the Land/ Fire, Fire, Fire/ A River of Stars', which Lim explains are the elemental themes of the work: 'the expressive vibrating body (the heart in the land or earth); transformation (fire); spiralling forms that open out towards a world beyond the human (River of Stars)'. These 'elemental themes' are suggested by some of the contrasting sections which go to make up the work, but don't dictate the overall structure in any simple sense.

As the chant comes to its close, the bassoon section (two standard instruments and one contrabassoon) builds up a mysterious texture punctuated by isolated sounds from claves and woodblocks, and the eerie sound produced by a cymbal placed on the timpani skin as the player manipulates its tension. Lim gradually overlays this with new lines – cor anglais and oboe, and lapidary figurations from piano. Above this the flautist enters on piccolo, initially with isolated single staccato notes, including the tritonal F-B which will have some significance throughout. The didjeridu player rattles a clapstick on the instrument (like the boomerang roll, a common gesture in Indigenous music to signal the beginning of a new section) and in response the piccolo takes up some of the repeated D sharps with which the chant began. Lim has noted how the low brass, bassoons and contrabassoon, bass and contrabass clarinet and double basses have a special prominence in the piece – 'they become a meta-didjeridu!' – but in fact the first extended passage of didjeridu solo is set off by a transparent texture of solo woodwinds and high violins.

Typically what happens in this piece is a gradual elaboration of material before a new section is introduced. Lim's image for this process is what she calls the 'branching song':

> These branches are full of iterations – shimmering woodwinds, radiant 'cicada' brass, whispers transforming into lyrical then distorted sounds in the strings, dynamic interventions from piano and percussion that merge into buzzing insect sounds and long drones. The aesthetic category of 'shimmer' that is so prized in Indigenous cultures comes into play in my thinking – musical textures like rippling water that sparkles in the light, the shimmering musical patterns that register the presence of an underlying structure (the chant) while simultaneously veiling it.

In the first section, the music is dominated by reiterated semiquaver patterns across the orchestral spectrum that contrast with a slower, heterophonic texture: chords are sounded in the winds and echoed by the strings who then elaborate them into short melodic motifs. The section closes with the chorale-like passage for brass mentioned above, where the harmony is relatively consonant – lots of perfect fourths and major seconds – set off against much faster figurations in woodwind, string and timpani parts. Elaborate solo lines are hushed by a striking unison E in the lowest wind parts and the first change from $\frac{4}{4}$ metre since the opening chant.

This ushers in a section where the flautist now plays the standard concert instrument. Here the flute writing makes more use of multiphonics and vocalisation against extremely high lines for strings and the sounds of two 'ocean drums' or *geophones* (rotating drums filled with sand – an invention of the late Olivier Messiaen). This instigates a gradual increase of 'breathy' sounds – such as whispering through the didjeridu, air blown through wind instruments without tone, very light left-hand pressure on strings – and an equally gradual attenuation of pitched sound. Against these sighs and whispers the bass flute emerges, and has a brief section with didjeridu alone. Pitched sounds, now in the pale form of string harmonics, provide a halo of sound interrupted by a flourish from the orchestral flutes and oboes, and short solo lines for viola and clarinet. But the breath sounds return, the whole orchestra making rhythmic respiring noises 'like giant wings opening and closing'. Lim's inspiration for this was a 'silent dance' performed by Aurukun people from Cape York in which 'the dancers silently moved their arms in unison guided by a silent inner song'. The importance of breath links the work to both Indigenous ritual and to Chinese music where, as Lim puts it, 'the breathing of instruments, the sounds in between sounds, are as important as a melodic phrase'.

From this still point, the music regains pitch and momentum, the repeated note figure from the chant occasionally providing an energetic ostinato through the texture and more elaborate swirling lines appearing in the woodwinds. The unison E precipitates out of the texture – this time for all brass and low woodwinds in a gesture reminiscent of Ligeti's *Lontano*. In a slightly faster tempo the music becomes more elaborate again with a rhythmic counterpoint for high winds and cellos and ebullient lines for solo piccolo, until another sudden hush where the note E is prominent.

The following section is dominated by birdcall-like patterns for piccolo and orchestral flutes while two sets of clapsticks and didjeridu set up an intricate interlocking pattern and rapid repeated three-note figures shimmer in the upper strings. These triplets migrate through bassoons, trumpets and high winds including solo piccolo, and the vibrant texture which follows supports a varied restatement of the brass 'chorale' mentioned earlier.

While this doesn't represent a 'climax' in any traditional sense, it marks the beginning of the music's move through a series of simpler textures (though with no lessening of the virtuosity of the solo parts). Repeated note motifs, recalling the chant, can be heard in the upper winds as, gradually, the orchestral players swap their instruments for toy 'insect clickers'. A slow whole-tone scale takes the cellos to the A above the treble stave, a wailing sound that might recall the Chinese *erhu*; this is answered by A in the depths of the wind section, recalling the texture with which the work began. Didjeridu and insect clickers evoke a universe beyond our human intuitions of time and space before silence falls again.

Chapter 5

Other (Australian) Landscapes

Australia is the most urbanised country on earth, in that a huge percentage of its citizens live in cities along the east coast; few of the landscapes that figure in Australian music are actually inhabited by the people who write the music, or for whom it is written. Much of Australia is flat and arid, and there are innumerable − in fact far too many − works by Australian composers which celebrate Uluru (formerly Ayers Rock), the striking megalith at the country's geographical heart. But the continent does of course contain many very different landscapes, and composers have also sought to depict these in music or to use them as the basis or setting for various works. Alfred Hill's *Linthorpe* portrays a specific site in the Blue Mountains near Sydney. In 1950, Margaret Sutherland composed one of her finest pieces, *Haunted*

Hills, a symphonic poem celebrating the Dandenong Ranges east of Melbourne and a work which, as she later put it in a radio interview, 'was all about the Aborigines'. Unusually for composers of his generation, Barry Conyngham decided early in his career that the city, rather than the empty landscape, was to generate much of his music. The title of his 1968 work *Crisis: Thoughts in a City* says it all; in the bicentennial ballet *Vast* the cities are treated as integral to the landscape, following on from *Monuments* in which Conyngham pairs iconic structures from the natural and built environments.

One of the most striking works to mark the bicentenary of white settlement in Australia was the opera *Whitsunday* with music by Brian Howard (born 1951) and libretto by Louis Nowra. It was his third major opera, and where the first two were both very internally focused – *Inner Voices* (also to a text by Nowra) begins in a dungeon with a mute as central character; *Metamorphosis* retells Kafka's story of a man transformed into an insect – *Whitsunday* recreates a kind of Shakespearean *Tempest* off the coast of Queensland. The intense psychological exploration is still there, but couched in music as colourful and vibrant as the physical backdrop of the tropical coast. Richard Mills' (born 1949) orchestral *Bamaga Diptych* was 'inspired by the experience of the transition from the dry to the wet season on Cape York'[1] at the far north of Queensland also, while Liza Lim responds to the Glasshouse Mountains in her cello work of the same name. The Barton/Hindson *Kalkadungu* mentioned earlier is 'set' in the Mount Isa region of the same state. Don Kay (born 1933) has produced several pieces which celebrate the island-state of Tasmania (which, lying at 40 degrees south is as far from the desert as you can get). His *Tasmania Symphony – The Legend of Moinee* tells in an attractive, almost Prokofievian, music the traditional story of Moinee, who, as Kay puts it in his program note, 'like Lucifer was hurled down' from the skies and who became a powerful ancestral spirit in the southern reaches of the island. Kay's love of Tasmania is further expressed in *There is an Island*, a large-scale work for children's choir and orchestra. Sculthorpe's early work, *The Fifth Continent*, took a broad view of the country, especially in such movements as 'Small Town', which derives from DH Lawrence's responses to the Illawarra coast near Sydney. Recently Sculthorpe has shifted his focus from the outback in works like *Kakadu* (which, like many of his works, uses the Aboriginal melody *Djilile* from Arnhem Land) and *Nourlangie*, both strongly rooted in the landscapes of the Top End. In recent years he has begun to re-examine his own Tasmanian heritage, and some of his own earliest music, in pieces like *Quamby* and *My Country Childhood* where neo-tonality meets neoteny.

The majority of works mentioned in this section have some kind of extra-musical relationship to landscape, and this is naturally the case in works which have a textual component. The poetry of Judith Wright, for instance, has been much set in songs by Australian composers from Margaret Sutherland to Richard Mills, and Ian Munro (born 1963) has not only set her words to music but used them as the generating ideas for abstract symphonic works. Like Barry Conyngham composers have also sought to represent the urban experience in music. Richard Mills used one of the most famous Australian plays, *The Summer of the Seventeenth Doll*, as the basis for his first major opera of the same name to a libretto by Peter Goldsworthy. Though it arguably lacked the mythic force that would have translated kitchen-sink drama into music, the piece did breathe a palpable sense of inner-city Melbourne in the 1950s. Mills followed this with *Batavia* (2001) (also with Goldsworthy) which tells the story of a Dutch shipwreck and the subsequent gruesome depravity of its passengers and crew off the coast of northern Australia: a powerful metaphor for the foundering of mercantile capitalism. Younger composers, not surprisingly, have explored the urban most assiduously. Stephen Adams' (born 1963) *Sydney Dreaming* is a choral work whose harmonies and textures are extremely evocative of that city in certain moods; Elliott Gyger (born 1968) used Kenneth Slessor's iconic poem *Five Bells*, set on Sydney Harbour, as the basis for his littoral orchestral meditation, *Deep and Dissolving Verticals of Light*, a work whose highly individual orchestration is enhanced by the unusual spatial layout of the orchestra on stage. The spirit of place reaches a post-modern[2] apotheosis in *The Eighth Wonder* (2000) with libretto by

Dennis Watkins and music by Alan John, being an opera about the Sydney Opera House in which the opera was being staged.

Another extra-musical theme that emerged in Australian music in the late 1960s and early 1970s is that of voyaging and exploration, partly, no doubt, as 1970 was the bicentenary of Captain Cook's landfall at Botany Bay. Sculthorpe wrote an opera about the Spanish explorer Quiros who was sure he had discovered the Southern Land of the Holy Spirit (he had actually landed in what is now Vanuatu – formerly the New Hebrides); Nigel Butterley (born 1935) wrote a piano concerto called *Explorations*; one of Richard Meale's works from this time is *Very High Kings* – the overture to a projected series of works about Christopher Columbus (an example of the pervasive Spanish influence on his work during that decade). As we have noted, the image of inland explorers like Leichhardt and Eyre have been important catalysts for works by Meale and Conyngham, and the figure in Conyngham's later work has morphed into that of the flawed visionary – the inventor Lawrence Hargrave (also the subject of an opera by Nigel Butterley) and the painter Brett Whiteley.

Landscape has continued to inform significant works of Australian music – understandably, given the many unique environments in this country. Some composers, of course, evoke the natural world in much more general terms: for instance, many of Ann Ghandar's (born 1943) exquisite piano works take their inspiration from rain and flowers, but her distinctive style makes these far more than merely descriptive. David Lumsdaine, as we will see, celebrates the forests of the coastline near Sydney. Sculthorpe's 'landscape music' since the late 1970s has tended to evoke everywhere but the central deserts: Kakadu and Jabiru in the Northern Territory, New Norcia in southern Western Australia. In *Mangrove* he brings together a varied number of imagined places.

Peter Sculthorpe: Picking up Shining Pearls

Strolling with his mother in the Melbourne Botanic Gardens at the age of nine, Peter Sculthorpe met the composer Percy Grainger and told him that he intended to be a composer too. 'My boy', Grainger exclaimed, 'you must look north, to the islands!'[3] Grainger's advice was sound and Sculthorpe clearly took it to heart. Much of his music has resulted from an interest in the music of Australia's neighbours, as well as from the impulse to bring together aspects of native Australian music with that of the heritage of the West.

Having beaten the path familiar to earlier generations of Australian musicians to Britain for further study, Sculthorpe returned to Australia in 1960. He soon established himself as a leading figure of his generation; works such as *The Fifth Continent* and the *Sun Music* series demonstrated his interest in writing music which reflects the cultural and environmental essence of his country. Sculthorpe's early career is discussed in some detail in Covell's *Australia's Music*; Graeme Skinner's recent biography, *Peter Sculthorpe: The Making of an Australian Composer*[4], charts the development of Sculthorpe's style and musical concerns from his early life until 1974. Suffice it to say that by the time Covell's book appeared, Sculthorpe had made his name with some of the works we've discussed previously – pieces that in some way reflect on what the expression 'Australian music' might mean. One of his first acknowledged pieces, *Irkanda I* for solo violin (1955) quite literally reflects the shape of the landscape around the city of Canberra, which sits in a wide valley in the foothills of the Great Dividing Range. The work's title means 'scrub country', a landscape that Sculthorpe came to associate with the image of a 'remote and lonely place'.

The 1960s also saw the *Sun Music* series for orchestra, where Sculthorpe harnessed some of the new sounds of the contemporary European avant-garde – cluster harmony, indeterminate pitch and extended instrumental techniques – to create a quite new musical language; the end of that decade saw his String Quartet No. 8, in which the sounds and rhythmic patterns of Balinese music were fundamental. The 1970s saw a variety of new works: *Love 200* for rock band and orchestra – an offering for the celebrations of the 1970 bicentenary of Captain Cook's arrival on the east coast of Australia; the ritual-opera *Rites of Passage* of 1974 (intended for the opening of the Sydney Opera House) and in 1977 *Port Essington*, a work in which musical imagery depicting the clash of European and Australian worlds is vividly imagined.

In 1968 Sculthorpe had been invited to visit Japan and it was there that he became acquainted with various aspects of traditional Japanese culture. After a short period in a Zen monastery, he spent time in a Shinto temple in Kyoto where the abbot introduced him to some of the traditional *saibara* chants, ancient melodies appropriated into the music of the Imperial court over some centuries. The *saibara* melody, *Ise-no-umi* would prove central to one of Sculthorpe's greatest orchestral scores, *Mangrove*, composed in 1979. Sculthorpe noted that Shinto's central deity is the sun goddess, and felt that by using such a chant in *Mangrove* he was effectively adding to the *Sun Music* corpus. The text of *Ise-no-umi (The sea of Ise)* reads:

> On the clean beach of Ise
> While the tide is low,
> Let's gather the seaweed,
> Let's gather the sea shells,
> Let's pick up shining pearls.

In *Mangrove* (1979), a work of simple eloquence, many of Sculthorpe's abiding interests are integrated, particularly his interest in specific Australian landscapes and the sounds and stories of cultures in Australia's geographical region. In his introduction to the score Sculthorpe outlines the imagery behind the music, referring to 'thoughts of Sidney Nolan's rain-forest paintings, in which Eliza Fraser and the convict Bracefell become, through love, birds and butterflies and Aboriginal graffiti'. Eliza Fraser was the wife of the captain of the *Sterling Castle*, wrecked off the Queensland coast in 1836. She was one of the few survivors who reached the island named after her by boat, all of whom (including her husband) perished. She was cared for by an escaped convict, who had gained the trust of the local Aborigines, but whom she betrayed when they finally reached a white settlement. Patrick White used the story as the basis for his 1973 novel *A Fringe of Leaves*, which in turn inspired composer Brian Howard's work of the same name for chorus and string orchestra in 1982. Sculthorpe had intended to use Fraser's story as the basis for a full-scale opera – Skinner's book details the development and eventual abandonment of the project. In the event, the monodrama *Eliza Fraser Sings* (to a libretto by Barbara Blackman) was completed in 1978. In addition to the Fraser story and its tropical setting, *Mangrove* also evokes 'recollections of a beach, mangrove-free, at Ise in Japan; and thoughts of a New Guinea tribe that believes man and woman to be descended from mangroves.'[5] Thus the natural environment of the Queensland coast is the setting for one of modern Australia's earliest love stories and human love is given a wider resonance by reference to the New Guinea creation myth and the sacred traditions of Japan.

Mangrove is, no pun intended, a watershed piece. Sculthorpe deliberately sought to purge his style of certain mannerisms: for instance, he omits woodwinds and harp so as to avoid what he considered the hackneyed sounds of water and rain. Very occasionally a semi-improvised flourish from vibraphone adds aquatic punctuation.

Formally, the work is much more seamless than some of his earlier, and indeed later, music. Sculthorpe often begins a new work by drawing up a plan in graphic form: almost all of his larger-scale works are accretions of self-contained sections. Very often, the music deliberately eschews anything like the western sense of development in favour of more static blocks of material; the drama is in the contrast from section to section. This is of course related to the sense of time that the composer wishes to create: like much non-western ritual music, or for that matter that of Messiaen, Sculthorpe's work often seems to exist outside of time as we often experience it. The use of the self-contained block of material, the repeated ostinato figure, and harmony that doesn't generate strongly differentiated moments of tension and repose all contrive to create a sense of time older than the time of chronometers. Like its predecessors, *Mangrove* is built up from clearly contrasting sections, but these are dovetailed, their edges blurred, and in the final minutes, material from those sections is combined vertically.

The opening section for brass and skin-drums is dominated by terse repetitions of two-note motifs, a reference to certain characteristic patterns in Balinese music. A repeated figure in the drums and trills from the brass give way to a contrastingly static series of muted string chords. Sculthorpe has noted that these sections are concerned with 'love and loving', and, as Michael Hannan[6] has pointed out, the pitch material of these richly inflected chords is very similar to that used by Messiaen where his music seeks to evoke human love. With minimal accompaniment of double basses and tuned percussion, the cellos then state a long section of *Ise-no-umi*. In an imaginative masterstroke, Sculthorpe divides the cello section and instructs one group to play deliberately 'out of step' (or as he puts it, *fuori di passo*) with each other. This technique is related to the heterophony of traditional Japanese music, where different instruments simultaneously play essentially the same melody but with different ornamentation and perhaps some variation of rhythm and metre – a kind of specious counterpoint; Sculthorpe uses a similar effect in the 'Lontano' ('far away') sections of his *Landscape II* for piano quartet which dates from about the same time and also uses Japanese material. The effect, in both cases, is of hearing the melody echoing in a space with a very long delay, like a cathedral. It also evokes the sounds of Gregorian chant. (Significantly, Sculthorpe used Gregorian chant to telling effect in his Requiem for solo cello, also written in 1979; there, hieratic chant melodies represent the formal aspects of the liturgy, contrasting with a more anxious personal idiom which reflects the voice of the individual soul.) A passage of random string sounds, evoking birdsong, briefly interrupts *Ise-no-umi*. The opening brass and drum texture returns in a more insistent mood, at first punctuated by short unpitched pizzicatos from the strings and then overlaid with the birdsong texture. The climax of the work is reached in a fuller statement of the 'love' music, now underpinned by the brass, before the horns and trombones, later joined by the trumpets and the strings, restate the Japanese melody, again creating the sense of limitless vistas.

David Lumsdaine: Wonder and Imagination

In 1989 David Lumsdaine spent two days in the forests of Cambewarra Mountain south of Sydney, where he recorded the extraordinary diversity of birdsong at different times of day. The CD *Cambewarra Mountain* was the first of three collections of soundscapes that Lumsdaine made for Tall Poppies Records; in his notes to the third, *Lake Emu*, he remarks on the 'rambling fantasy to their music, an inconsequentiality shared by most of the birdsong this warm morning'.[7] In his soundscape recordings the rambling fantasy of birdsong becomes the building blocks for rigorous composition. The distinctive elements act like thematic material in a work for human voices or instruments. As we've noted, in their formal poise Lumsdaine's soundscapes make an interesting contrast with the equally engaging but deliberately more raw and anarchic *Currawong* recordings by Moya Henderson.

The sounds and landscapes of Australia struck Lumsdaine with particular force when he returned to this country in 1973 after 20 years in the UK. Educated in Sydney, Lumsdaine had travelled to Britain in 1952 for further study with Lennox Berkeley and Mátyás Seiber; the latter provided a link to the developments in the music of the European avant-garde whose techniques Lumsdaine absorbed. He withdrew much of the music composed before the mid-1960s, with *Annotations of Auschwitz* (to a text by expatriate poet Peter Porter) his first acknowledged work. In 1966 he produced *Kelly Ground*, signalling two important aspects of his subsequent work: a renewed interest in his home country – the Kelly in question is, of course, the bushranger Ned – and the use of the 'ground', a repeating pattern which supports the elaboration of a piece, as a structuring principle.

Australian landscapes had been important to Lumsdaine's aesthetic before his return – the *Aria for Edward John Eyre* was completed in the months before – but he describes the shock of seeing them again as enormous. A major work written in the aftermath of that visit, *Salvation Creek with Eagle*, shows the composer's intense love for a particular patch of the Ku-ring-gai Chase National Park, its colours, warmth and birdsong, though as Lumsdaine puts it: 'The music is not about these things; they are where the music came from.'[8]

This is a crucial aspect of Lumsdaine's relationship to landscape: he is not about creating music analogues for visual imagery (even though his use of natural sound is in fact much more literal than, say, Sculthorpe, whose birdsong episodes are ciphers or symbols rather than quotations or representations). As in *Cambewarra Mountain*, Lumsdaine's use of the material involves shaping and formalising. It's no surprise, then, that his works should include a series of pieces entitled *Mandala*. In Sanskrit *mandala* means circle; it has come to refer to the often ornate images which function as objects on which to meditate. These are usually based on a circle which carries a radiating system of intricate, symmetrical patterns representing the cosmos.[9] In Tantric iconography the centre is often a single point, representing the ultimate singularity of the universe; some Buddhist mandalas include a representation of the Buddha at the centre. The mind, by concentrating on these abstract patterns, can free itself from distraction.

Lumsdaine came to the idea of the mandala in 1967 when he was 'watching the play of light on the patterns of sandbanks and water sculptured by the receding tide on the Kent coast; the play became a dance, and over the next few days the dance became a mandala for wind quintet'.[10] So in contrast to some of his Australian colleagues, Lumsdaine was not setting about to create 'Asian' music: as he goes on to explain, the defining character of his *Mandala* series is 'the single-minded way each has grown from a brief, central musical image into a diversity of transformed song shapes'. Not that Lumsdaine hasn't explored aspects of Asian cultures in his work. The large-scale work *Hagoromo* for orchestra is inspired by an incident in a Japanese *Nōh* play where an angel dances for two fishermen who have found and returned her robe. Lumsdaine's music makes no attempt to sound Japanese and yet in its iridescent weaving of rapidly moving winds and harp lines he creates an imaginary Japan not unlike that of Brian Howard's *The Temple of the Golden Pavilion* composed a few years later. But Lumsdaine's cultural interests are catholic, encompassing mandalas, *Nōh* drama, jazz, the sounds of the Australian bush and the tradition of western music and art going back to the Middle Ages. His cello concerto, *The Garden of Earthly Delights*, takes its title and form from the famous hellish imagery of Hieronymus Bosch; the solo cantata, *A tree telling of Orpheus*, sets an unusual and moving account of the Greek myth by the Welsh-American poet Denise Levertov, where a tree describes both the joy and the agony of wrenching itself from the ground to follow the legendary singer.

The natural world, then, is of supreme importance to this composer as a source of 'wonder and imagination'. *Mandala I*, as we've noted, grew out of that precise moment of observation on the coast; *Mandala V*, for orchestra, similarly derives from a precise location. The series, incidentally, was not planned that way: in fact the composer only gives a work that title if, in the course of the composition, it reveals itself to behave in that 'single-minded way'. *Mandala II (Catches Catch)*, for flute, clarinet, percussion, viola and cello, appeared a year after the first, in 1969; *Mandala III*, for solo piano, flute, clarinet, viola, cello and bell, nearly a decade later in 1978; and *Mandala IV*, for string quartet, in 1983.

Mandala V was commissioned by the ABC for the Sydney Symphony and premiered in 1989. The score is prefaced by a short verse:

> rocks, roots embrace –
> the angophora grows out of
> the sandstone cliff

to which in his notes Lumsdaine adds 'early spring, full moon, an hour before sunrise. This is the centre of my mandala.' The setting is, of course, the coastal forests of the Sydney Basin, where large, smooth-barked, salmon-coloured angophora trees grow into fantastic shapes, preaching, as James McAuley put it, 'with the gestures of Moses'.[11] And these forests are home to a variety of birds, whose calls hanging in crisp pre-dawn air cast the first spell in this piece.

Lumsdaine's palette in this work is a model of orchestration. He conjures the pre-dawn world out of surprisingly little material: simple

David Lumsdaine: *Mandala V*, bars 19–21. Lumsdaine's writing
for three clarinets evokes the dawn chorus of currawongs. Used by
permission of the composer.

harp chords, insect and bird calls from marimba and flute. A trio of
clarinets sounds like a group of currawongs (see music example); a
group of five solo violins and glockenspiel creates the kind of glittering
dawn chorus that Messiaen evokes from birdsong in a similar passage
in his *Chronochromie*, a micropolyphony of rapidly repeated notes and
wide-leaping gestures. For the first five minutes or so Lumsdaine draws
these delicate textures from small groups within the orchestra: pairs
of oboes, a mournful tuba. A gorgeous wash of sound from the whole
orchestra introduces what the composer calls a chorale: a series of
chords which form the 'ground' of the piece. In baroque music the
'ground' is a bass line, repeated in forms like the passacaglia with ever
more ornate variations superimposed on each repetition. Like Brahms
in his Symphony No. 4, or Shostakovich in the Piano Trio No. 2,
Lumsdaine's use of chords gives the work a harmonic unity, and the
unfolding of the work is a process of teasing out the implications of
the harmony. Having stated the chordal material, Lumsdaine can then
explode it into an inexhaustible array of colours and textures which
he does through a variety of methods, including the medieval technique of isometric canon, where material is presented simultaneously

at different speeds. For him 'there was a kind of structural metaphor', a correspondence between 'the way the isometric canons shaped, twisted and refined [the material] and the drowned valleys of the Hawkesbury River'.[12] The overwhelming effect of this piece is of a constant, iridescent shimmer.

A crucial difference between a pictorial mandala and a work of music is, of course, that the latter takes place in time, so any sense of symmetry is an illusion. The first movement of Bartók's *Music for Strings, percussion and celesta* is a case in point: in order to sound like a piece reaching its apogee and then going into reverse, the second half is in fact shorter and more compressed – it would otherwise seem too long. Lumsdaine's piece has a similarly arch-shaped structure: the central sections of the piece are where the most forceful tutti sections occur, as well as particularly thrilling passages such as those for ecstatically high trumpets. An especially climactic section occurs just before the work's coda, as it might in any classical piece. Lumsdaine describes it as a 'vigorous dance which fuses with the chorale', and it is here that the implications of the chorale become explicitly stated at the same time as the more intricate foreground that characterises the work. In a reminiscence, rather than a recapitulation, the currawong/clarinets return in the work's final pages, ushering in a final gentle statement of unadorned material from the chorale in the strings and woodwinds. Lumsdaine compares this reestablishment to an effect of 'perspective – as the chorale moves into "ordinary" time at the end of the work, the larger landscape refines into the particular tree'.[13]

Like many works in the 'Australian landscape' genre, *Mandala V* is a meditation 'on the composer's experience – vision – of particular places in the natural world'[14] and is one of the finest of its type. Lumsdaine's musical language is given a distinctly Australian flavour not by abstract notions of landscape but by a creative response to the actual sounds of birdsong, which he uses as the basis for rigorously developed large-scale structures and beguilingly beautiful textures.

Chapter 6

Dreaming of Asia

... sea-shades and sky-shades,
Like umbrellas in Java.

Wallace Stevens, 'Tea' (1923)

The notion of exploration, discussed earlier in 'Other (Australian) Landscapes', perhaps accounts for Australians' interest in the music and, more broadly, culture of neighbouring countries in the 1960s. Japan and the Indonesian regions of Bali and Java attracted particular attention and this established an ongoing strand in Australian art music. Curiously, though, where composers enthusiastically studied and replicated the music of these areas, other cultures in the region were largely ignored. Our composers have shown relatively little interest in the music of Melanesian countries like our nearest neighbour,

Papua New Guinea, or of Polynesian culture. It has fallen to composers like David Bridie, working in the popular music and film area, to explore and record the music of Papua New Guinea and the Solomon and Trobriand Islands. A significant exception in the art music area is Martin Wesley-Smith (born 1945), whose crusading on behalf of the people of East Timor has generated notable works, beginning with *Kdadalak*, a powerful multi-media work based on poetry by Francisco Borja da Costa, who died during Indonesia's invasion of East Timor in 1975. More recently Wesley-Smith's opera *Quito* (1994) to a libretto by his brother Peter, explores the tragedy of a young East Timorese schizophrenic man who died by his own hand in Darwin in 1987.

Sculthorpe's exposure to Japanese music is clearly reflected in *Music for Japan* which he wrote for the Australian Youth Orchestra's tour of that country in 1970, and which contains several gestures immediately intelligible to an audience familiar with classical Japanese theatre: the distinctive opening drum figure, for instance, recalls the signal that the show is about to start. He further, and perhaps more beautifully, refined a Japanese sensibility in the piano pieces *Snow, Moon and Flowers* (1971), which pianist Roger Woodward has recorded – plucking the piano strings to give the instrument a koto-like timbre. And as we've seen, in *Mangrove* (1979) Sculthorpe uses a whole Japanese melody so that his piece is infused by its characteristics, such as the gapped scale which emphasises the intervals of the major third and falling semitone.

Sculthorpe's contemporary, Richard Meale, wrote a number of pieces inspired by the Japanese *haiku* poet, Bashō, while also shaking things up with works inspired by slightly subversive European poets like Arthur Rimbaud and Federico García Lorca. Meale, unlike Sculthorpe, was never particularly interested in writing music that sounded like its non-European models. Where Sculthorpe will quote whole melodies, as in *Mangrove*, Meale takes an aesthetic image or idea as the starting point for his own musical elaboration. For Meale, the nationality of the poetry of Bashō, Rimbaud or Lorca is secondary to their value to his imagination. One of Meale's greatest large-scale works, *Images*

– *Nagauta* (1966), reflects the formal dramatic structure, rather than the sound-world, of a certain kind of *kabuki* play; the short orchestral piece *Clouds now and then* (1969) is an exquisite response to one of Bashō's more striking poems. Bashō's poetry has also figured in works by Roger Smalley like *The Narrow Road to the Deep North* (1983) and Barry Conyngham who, as we have noted, went to Japan for further study in 1970. The result, that year, was his first major work, *Ice Carving* for amplified violin and strings, a musical representation of the huge ice sculptures carved in the grounds of the Imperial Palace in Tokyo each winter. *As I Crossed a Bridge of Dreams* (1975), arguably the masterpiece of Conyngham's contemporary Anne Boyd (born 1946), is a largely text-less series of three meditations on dreams recorded by the eleventh-century Lady Sarashina; its striking textures for unaccompanied choir derive in part from the composer's interest in the sound of the *sho*, or Japanese mouth organ. Vincent Plush's (born 1950) early work for solo flute, *Cho no mai* (1973) refers to a maiden's dance in *Nōh* theatre.

Increasingly we hear in the music of the 1960s and 1970s sounds derived from the *gamelan*. The gamelan exists in a variety of forms in different parts of the Indonesian archipelago. In Bali, a still largely Hindu community, the gamelan retains some links with religious ritual; in other parts of Muslim Indonesia its role is still ceremonial but rather more secular. Typically, the gamelan is an orchestra of tuned and untuned percussion instruments, where the former weave an elaborate polyphony out of particular modes – usually of five or seven notes (the 'black-note' pentatonic scale is only one kind of five-note mode). Large-scale musical paragraphs are articulated by what is known as the 'gong cycle'. The gamelan's intricate foreground and largely static substructure were extremely attractive to composers who were deliberately trying to avoid the goal-directed techniques of western music. Sculthorpe became interested in the music of Bali in the late 1960s, spurred on by the publication in 1966 of Colin McPhee's *Music in Bali*, the first systematic examination of Balinese music by a westerner. (The distinctive sounds and rhythmic structures of the Balinese gamelan had, of course, been seeping into western music since the time of Debussy, who famously described its polyphony as richer than that of Palestrina.) This bore its first fruits, in Sculthorpe's work, in what is now known as *Sun Music III* (1967) and in the String Quartet No. 8 (1969). In *Angklung* (1974) Anne Boyd evokes that gentle Balinese instrument using only a four-note scale in a wonderfully meditative piece for solo piano; her *Bencharong* (1976) for string orchestra is a strikingly beautiful contemplation of the sonorities made possible by the simple interval of the major second. Boyd's experience of living and working in Hong Kong for many years fuelled her creative response to east Asian music in works like *Meditation on a Chinese Character* and her collaboration with the Korean-Australian poet Don'o Kim produced song-cycles such as *My Name is Tian* (1979) and *Cycle of Love* (1981).

The music and culture of the Asia-Pacific region has remained important in the work of younger composers, particularly those who were students of either Sculthorpe or of the generation he himself taught. It has also generated significant works from outside that sphere. Larry Sitsky, for instance, was born in China in 1934 to Russian Jewish parents and remembers hearing indigenous music in his home town of Tianjin. Sitsky has ranged extraordinarily widely in his interests, including responding to the ancient Chinese system of divination in his Violin Concerto No. 3, *I Ching* (1987) and to the Hindu concept of constant reincarnation in the chamber work *Samsara*. (He has more recently essayed Aboriginal music in his Violin Concerto No. 4 – which has the giveaway subtitle of 'Dreaming'.) In the 1980s Melbourne composer Peter Tahourdin (born 1928) likewise immersed himself in Indian music to produce works in the *Raga Music* series – notably not attempting to sound like classical Indian music, and setting such non-subcontinental poets as Gerard Manley Hopkins in the first of the series (1985). And, demonstrating that Japan isn't all cherry blossoms and tea ceremonies, Brian Howard's powerful *The Temple of the Golden Pavilion* (1978) enacts the psychotic story of the same name by Yukio Mishima in an opulent but appropriately acerbic orchestral idiom. Vincent Plush, who eschewed Asian influence after *Cho no mai*, has in a number of works looked as far afield as South America. His major orchestral suite *Pacifica* (1987) is a homage to various cultures around the Pacific rim and on its scattered archipelagos.

Inevitably much Asian-influenced music is 'Orientalist' in the sense decried by the late Edward Said[1]: it portrays an Asia far removed from present day, or even past, realities – moon viewing and pearl gathering have nothing much to do with invasion, famine or carpet-bombing. (It need not be stressed that the same criticism can be levelled at composers who appropriate elements of Aboriginal culture.) It creates a 'dream world' where the virtues of stasis, gentleness and repetition are cultivated, but essentially unmoored from their cultural, often formal, context; furthermore, much of the Japanese poetry so admired by Australian composers was, like the paintings of Vermeer, a triumph of serenity and form in a world of chaos and brutality. This distance from context can be seen in Sculthorpe's program note to *Koto Music* (1976) for piano and tape: he describes that importance of Japanese scales and playing techniques, then states that 'although *Koto Music* stems from Japanese ideas, I believe that the work, through its repeated tones and sense of space, has in it much of the feeling of the Australian landscape'.[2] The use of surface details might account for the frequent criticism of much Asian-influenced work: that it sounds like travelogue music. More strikingly, composers have begun not merely to respond in western music media to Asian music, but to start composing new work for traditional instruments. This partly results from the emergence of resourceful performers such as Riley Lee, a grand master of the *shakuhachi* (the end-blown Japanese flute) or Satsuki Odamura, a wonderful koto player. Composers like Sarah de Jong (born 1952), Conyngham and Lim have written especially for Odamura. In 1997 Ian Cleworth founded TaikOz as an offshoot of the Synergy Percussion ensemble to cultivate Japanese *taiko* drumming. The performances on huge drums have a sheer energy and power that balances any sense of Japanese music as being slow, quiet and 'refined'. And the world saw and heard just how well such elements have been brought together in Australian music when Ross Edwards' *Dawn Mantras*, featuring children's choir,

Graham Hilgendorf from the TaikOz ensemble. Photo by Bridget Elliot.

shakuhachi and didjeridu, was performed and telecast live from the sails of the Sydney Opera House on the morning of 1 January 2000.

In keeping too with the kind of society modern Australia is, a list of our most important composers includes people of Asian heritage. Lim is one, and has celebrated that aspect of her heritage in such pieces as *Yuè lìng jié* ('Moon spirit feasting' 1997–99) which she describes as a 'ritual street opera', and *Ming qi* ('Bright vessel' 2000) for oboe and percussion. Julian Yu, born in China but resident in Australia since 1985, has likewise explored Chinese aesthetics in his diaphanously beautiful *Hsiang-wen* ('Filigree clouds' 1990) for orchestra and, more disturbingly, the chamber opera *Fresh Ghosts* (1997). Moreover, Australian composers are more than ever engaging with the contemporary music of Asia, as much as with the continent's 'classical' traditions.

David Young (born 1969) is director of Aphids, a company devoted to the presentation of new music and, importantly, collaborative works across several media such as film and sculpture. Young's music is enriched by an ongoing relationship with Japanese music and ideas, and represents a fruitful incorporation of these with the language of European late modernism. Young has a fine ear for delicate sound created by microtonal pitching, harmonics, unconventional tuning of instruments and extended vocal and instrumental techniques. His song cycle *Thousands of Bundled Straw* is an amalgam of influences derived from the legend of Yoichi, who discovered a miraculous statue of the Buddha floating in the sea. The statue told Yoichi that if he jumped off a cliff his blind mother's sight would be restored, so he wrapped himself in bundles of straw and jumped; his mother regained her sight and he founded the Temple of the Healing Eyes above Lake Shinji. Into this work for soprano and mixed ensemble, Young weaves music which also reflects on the work of European writers Italo Calvino and Georges Perec. The title is a direct quotation from a 'Japlish' translation of the legend available at the Temple; as Young explains, 'the slight shift in grammar creates a small gap, a fissure into which meaning might slip unexpectedly'.[3] That is certainly the effect of his allusive and beautiful work.

The music and culture of Melanesia and Polynesia has, as we've noted, been less influential despite the explorations of Alfred Hill mentioned earlier. However, one of the initial images behind Sculthorpe's *Mangrove* is a Papuan creation myth (though the thematic material is largely derived from a Japanese melody). The New Zealand-born composer Gillian Whitehead (born 1941), for many years resident in Sydney, has turned to Maori myth in beautifully crafted chamber works such as *Manutaki* (1986); Maria Grenfell, born in 1969 in Malaysia, raised in New Zealand and now resident in Hobart, has likewise 'retold' Maori tales in works like *Hinemoa* (2007) for orchestra. Since 2003 the Trans-Tasman Exchange program, an initiative of the Australian Music Centre and its opposite number, SOUNZ, has made it possible for composers from one side of the creek to work with musicians on the other.

The response of Australian composers to the musics of the Asia-Pacific region has thus been varied. It includes simple replication of certain surface details, such as the use of pentatonic or other 'gapped' modes, static harmony and instrumental timbres which approximate those of non-western instruments. Other composers have taken to using those instruments either alone or in combination with instruments from other traditions. Another group has used particular aspects of a non-western culture as the starting point for work which remains more firmly within the western tradition.

Barry Conyngham and the Afterimage

Until the late 1960s Australian music's love affair with Asian culture had been largely mediated, as in the case of Sculthorpe's interest in Balinese music being sparked by Colin McPhee's research rather than first-hand experience. At the same time as Asian music was being embraced by Australians, a composer in Japan was bringing together the two traditions in much the same way. This was T ru Takemitsu (1930–1996), whose earliest works, such as the *Requiem for Strings* (1957) were decidedly western in their musical language. (That is not to say unoriginal, though: the *Requiem* was much praised by Stravinsky.) But in 1967 he produced *November Steps*, one of the first works to successfully blend traditional Japanese instruments like the shakuhachi and *biwa* (a four-stringed lute) with the western symphony orchestra. In 1968 Sculthorpe visited Japan and met Takemitsu; the Japanese composer visited Australia a year later and met Sculthorpe's circle of friends and students. Among them was Barry Conyngham, whose subsequent decision to use his Churchill Fellowship for travel to Tokyo (rather than London) in 1970 was, as we know, front-page news at the time.

It was the year of Expo 70, the world's fair in the city of Osaka (and a first for Asia) which had the idealistic motto of 'Progress and Harmony for Mankind'. Australia was represented there by the striking architecture of James Maccormick, where a huge cantilever shaped (deliberately) to resemble the great wave of Hokusai's famous print held a floating, lotus-shaped steel crown above the pavilion; Barry Conyngham composed music to be played inside the pavilion. The message was clear: Australia was a modern, technologically advanced society, open to the ideas and aesthetics – traditional and contemporary – of Asia. It was, therefore, a propitious time for a young Australian composer to be there.

Satsuki Odamura, koto virtuoso, for whom many Australian composers including Barry Conyngham have written. Photo by Christabelle Baranay.

Ice Carving and *Water ... Footsteps ... Time ...* were the first fruits of Conyngham's period with Takemitsu, and both reflect the latter's influence and aspects of traditional Japanese culture. On his return to Australia, however, Conyngham at first pursued specifically Australian themes in *Edward John Eyre*, *Voss* (not to be confused with Meale's opera), *Ned* (a music theatre work about the famous bushranger) and *The Apology of Bony Anderson* about the dehumanising effect of brutal imprisonment on an early Australian convict. In his instrumental works too Conyngham explores Australian landscapes: the concerto for violin and piano, *Southern Cross*, is in part a meditation on the sheer scale of

the continent; for the Bicentenary of white settlement, Conyngham composed the ballet score *Vast* which begins in the sea, traverses the interior, and concludes in the city; the keyboard concerto *Monuments* pairs iconic landmarks of the natural and built environments. Music theatre works from the 1980s likewise dramatise Australian stories, like that of Lawrence Hargrave, the aviator/inventor/explorer who is the hero of the opera *Fly*, and *Bennelong*, a puppet opera about the Sydney Cove Aborigine befriended by Governor Arthur Phillip. A major recurring theme in Conyngham's work is that of isolation[4], though this can be against a backdrop of urban energy as much as desert stillness.

In 1994 Conyngham composed *Afterimages* for bass koto and small orchestra to a commission from Satsuki Odamura. The title, as Conyngham has noted, refers to:

the phenomenon that we all experience after looking for a while at a bright object. As we look away an after image remains, projected over the next thing we look at. In this case the 'afterimages' are the memories I still carry of the time that I spent in Japan studying with Tōru Takemitsu ... This piece also acts as a meeting place of my long-term investigation of musical materials that attempt to dwell upon the Australian condition − a sense of space, isolation, yearning and restlessness − with the musical materials of Japan − music existing 'inside' the sound, rhythmic intensity, simple beautiful melodies.[5]

The koto is essentially a long zither, whose strings are stretched over movable bridges (allowing for flexible tuning) and struck by ivory plectrums worn on three fingers of each hand. The traditional instrument has thirteen strings, but over the last century a number of larger instruments have been developed. Of these only the *jūshichi-gen*, or seventeen-string koto, has been taken up. This was invented in 1921 by Michiko Miyagi, and is the instrument required in this work. It is sometimes referred to as a bass koto which is not entirely accurate though it does have greater resonance than the standard instrument, and Conyngham underlines this in the gesture which opens and frequently punctuates the texture: as a quick up-and-down glissando over the range of the instrument comes to rest on its lowest note, double bass and trombone sound the same pitch, so it's as if the koto has been strummed in a cavernous space.

This gesture also sets up the harmonic 'background' of the piece. The koto is traditionally tuned to one of several possible pentatonic scales; Conyngham's music, by contrast, relies on what he calls 'modulating scales'. In any traditional mode or scale, the pattern of pitches is identical from one octave to the next. A modulating scale changes as it rises, so that, for instance, an A natural in one octave may be altered to an A flat in the next. Any chord that is spread over more than one octave is

The opening of Barry Conyngham's *Afterimages* showing how his rich string harmony dissolves into woodwind figurations. Used by permission of the composer.

Afterimages

for Koto and Orchestra

for Satsuki

Barry Conyngham

therefore likely to contain what diatonic harmony calls 'simultaneous false relations' – in other words, a dissonance which gives each chord its distinct flavour. (See music example.) For example, the first chord in this piece, from the bass up, is: G flat, F, G sharp, A sharp, E, A natural; it is sounded by the strings (the upper parts in harmonics, way above), and decorated by arpeggiated, or broken, versions in alto flute and clarinet, to which the koto adds an ostinato pattern of repeated pairs of semiquavers. This is a common imprint of Conyngham's style, where the harmony is reinforced by melodic patterns that use the same notes and intervals; here he goes one step further by tuning the koto in such a way that it can etch out the rich harmony of the work. In other sections there is the pervasive use of a motif whose initially wide intervals gradually tighten around the narrow semitone; at one striking point the piccolo, in octaves with the koto, spins this out into a long and beautiful melody.

The timbre of the instrument inevitably conjures a musical image of Japan, even if the harmony is closer to the post-impressionist lushness of Messiaen and Takemitsu. In consultation with Odamura, Conyngham did include some 'extended techniques' imported from western contemporary music: the koto player must occasionally pluck or strum behind the bridges, giving an indeterminate pitch; the score calls for harmonics, produced as on a harp. As Conyngham makes clear in his program note, the work grows out of the twin impulse to evoke certain aspects of Japanese aesthetics as well as those qualities he sees as distinctly Australian. These don't equate to separate musical sections, though the work is built up of contrasting paragraphs. Some cultivate a shimmering stasis through the doubling of tremolando chords on koto and marimba, others have a rhythmic insistence where, for example, koto and string players are asked to tap their instruments percussively to 'amplify' the bongos against a blur of woodwind figurations. After a cadenza for koto and a reminiscence of the work's opening, Conyngham closes this piece with mysterious sounds created by shakuhachi-like breathiness in the winds, muted strings and brass, and unconventional use of metal percussion.

The first version of this piece was for just koto and percussion (1993), making the orchestral version an afterimage of an afterimage, perhaps. In neither case does the work attempt to sound like traditional Japanese music. It is rather a genuine fusion of traditional and contemporary sounds, of Asian and western aesthetics. Conyngham's work has continued its engagement with Japanese music until the present in works like *Dreams go wandering still* (2003) and *Now that darkness* (2004), and, most movingly, *Passing* (1998) − a tribute to his mentor Takemitsu.

Brian Howard and the Resonant Silence

Construction of the Kinkakuji or Golden Pavilion in the Japanese city of Kyoto began in 1397. It was built for Ashikaga Yoshimitsu, who reigned as *sh gun* for four decades from 1368. He abdicated, technically speaking, in favour of his son in 1394 and lived the life of a Zen Buddhist monk in his final years (though in reality managed also to maintain an iron grip on power until his death in 1408). After his death the building was converted into a temple, housing relics of the Buddha. It survived the upheavals of the next few centuries, including World War II − the historical significance of Kyoto was such that it was never bombed by the Allies. In 1950, however, the temple was deliberately burned to the ground by a young acolyte who had intended to die in the blaze but who lost his nerve and escaped. When he was captured and tried it emerged that the young man, physically unprepossessing and with a stammer, had grown to envy and hate the beauty and perfection of the temple. It was rebuilt in 1955 and in 1956 the young Japanese novelist Yukio Mishima published *The Temple of the Golden Pavilion*, his fictionalised account of the acolyte's developing obsession and anger.

Mishima's protagonist, Mizoguchi, is emotionally damaged by the experience of seeing his mother commit adultery in the presence of his dying father; the stammer is a direct result, and it in turn makes him a figure of derision throughout his childhood. As a student he is ridiculed by a beautiful young soldier who has returned to visit his old school and humiliated by a girl he tries to befriend; as an acolyte at the temple his attempts to attain purity are undermined by his friendship with the cynical Kashiwagi, but his attempts at debauchery are themselves undermined by the image of the temple in his mind. Mizoguchi's youth coincides with the war years, and at the war's end he has a startling epiphany while gazing at the temple. Up until then:

> the temple, its various parts and its whole structure had resounded with a sort of musical harmony. But what I heard this time was complete silence, complete noiselessness. Nothing flowed there, nothing changed. The Golden Temple stood before me, towered before me, like some terrifying pause in a piece of music, like some resonant silence.[6]

At that moment Mizoguchi understands that he and beauty exist in mutually exclusive worlds, 'a condition that will never improve so long as this world endures'.

Howard's *The Temple of the Golden Pavilion* is his second major orchestral score. His first, *Il Tramonto della Luna* ('The setting of the moon') appeared in 1976 and garnered its composer the highest award in the 1976 Trieste International Competition for Symphonic Composition. That work is based on a late poem by Giacomo Leopardi, in which he laments the inexorable passing of youth: moonlight is a symbol for the memory of youth; unlike the natural world, the ageing man will not be renewed by the coming sunlight of morning. At around this time too, Howard's first opera *Inner Voices*, to a libretto by Louis Nowra, premiered in Melbourne. His second opera, which appeared a few years later, used Stephen Berkoff's dramatisation of Kafka's famous *Metamorphosis*.

There is an interesting thread here. *Inner Voices* tells the story of a practically autistic young man who is groomed by an unscrupulous soldier to become a puppet Czar of Russia, and who inevitably comes to use – violently on occasion – the power he has been given. In *Metamorphosis* Gregor Samsa famously awakes one morning to find himself transformed into a giant insect. The narrator of Leopardi's poem faces unavoidable ageing and death; Mizoguchi is trapped by his ugliness and his stutter and his rage seeks and finds an apocalyptic outlet. Each of these figures is somehow trapped, and Howard's interest is in examining and dramatically depicting extreme psychological states that result.

Brian Howard composed his symphonic response to Mishima's novel in 1979. It is thus a direct contemporary of works by two of his teachers, Sculthorpe's *Mangrove* and Meale's *Viridian*. Both of those are in a sense examples of orientalist impressionism; both are watershed works for their composers and for the broader context of Australian music, and the same could be said for Howard's piece. At a time when images of Asia featured strongly in Australian music, it was a stark reminder that Asian aesthetics and culture are not merely decorative, and that 'Asian spirituality' could, like its counterpart in the West, develop a perverse and violent underside. It was, moreover, a work which is defiantly 'maximalist' in its musical language and use of orchestral timbre.

The Temple of the Golden Pavilion is not programmatic in the sense that we would use the word of Richard Strauss' *Ein Heldenleben*; there is no sense that the musical events are direct depictions of events in the novel. Rather, the composer has set himself an unusual challenge: to create in music both a sense of the perfect beauty of the temple itself and the inexorable slide of Mizoguchi's spirit into uncontrollable and destructive malice.

Howard achieves the sense of beauty in the first instance through his wonderfully imaginative use of orchestral colour. The arresting opening is characterised by bells articulating the attack of gleaming wind chords; the brass instruments snarl in fast, aggressively tangled figurations, adumbrating the violence which is to come. The texture lightens, with ornate figures for woodwinds and harps punctuated by isolated chimes and single-note gestures from horns. Repeated high chords from the strings create a sense of pulsing restlessness; a short plaintive gesture for oboe and harp is swept away by implacable fully scored chords before another passage of intricate polyphony for woodwinds, harp and celesta. Gradually, long trumpet notes, offering a promise of ecstasy, are introduced but undermined by brass writing made more acerbic by the use of flutter-tongue. This gives onto another passage of polyphony, now dominated by the obsessive plucking of pizzicato strings, whose dry timbre is emphasised by the sound of the marimba.

Quiet wind trills fade in over the marimba, with the incisive staccato brass chords briefly intruding before the texture is further enriched with string glissandos. Ghostly pulsing chords reassert themselves, again with isolated bell tones and harp figurations (one characteristic use of the harp in this work is the striking and immediate dampening of chords in its bass register, quite different from its more usual role in orchestral texture). The brass stacks itself into more highly dissonant chords, often adding the mocking laughter of rapid repeated notes at the end of each one. As their syncopations become more insistent, the timpani asserts itself in wide-ranging figurations, but the tension subsides with a texture of single flutter-tongued notes from the brass working in hocket, answering each other like birds in a forest.

Harp and ghostly string chords are heard again, but this delicacy does not last long, as a series of brass chords, moving upwards in a kind of chorale and then in isolated blasts, frame a virtuosic outburst from the timpani, answered by frenetic pizzicato and incisive wind chords. The harmonic rhythm is by this stage moving fast, as if to suggest the conflagration. With a final body-blow from the orchestra, the sound of bells is left to hang and dissolve on the air, 'a resonant silence'.

Without wanting to be too schematic, we might then suggest that 'beauty' is represented by the intricate, colourful and ever-changing textures that Howard draws from a huge number of small combinations from within the orchestra. There are moments of iridescent activity and serene suspense, but with violence lurking or expressed, particularly in the aggressive writing for brass. Formally, the music conveys the sense of inevitable disaster by its pitch organisation. The composer has used expressions like 'self-perpetuating pitch constellations'[7] or 'cyclical hierarchical pitch systems' to describe his harmonic practice. Neither is as scary as it sounds: the latter (which could apply to a 12-bar blues or Pachelbel's Canon) is possibly most helpful here. *The Temple of the Golden Pavilion* is punctuated by a series of 12 seven-note chords that articulate the music into those discrete textural sections that I've described. Each chord determines the prevailing harmony – those notes which are used more often or emphatically than others, and the relationship of chord to chord gives the music its onward momentum. The harmonic rhythm – time between changes of harmony – is relatively slow in this music, despite the foreground detail being often highly busy and ornate. As I have mentioned, though, this speed increases as the piece nears its end; the composer has by this time established the relationship of chord structures in the listener's ear, so that the effect is inevitable and dramatically shattering.

A career in education in Australia and Singapore meant that Howard's works were heard less often than they might have been. In 2008, however, he was appointed composer in residence with The Queensland Orchestra. For TQO he has composed a series of new pieces, among them *Earthshine* and *Gravity's Rainbow*. Both are masterfully scored, more opulent perhaps than *The Temple of the Golden Pavilion*, but with the same constant flux of gorgeous sound.

Chapter 7

Dreaming of Europe

The tenure of Eugene Goossens (1893–1962) at the Sydney Conservatorium and Sydney Symphony Orchestra between 1947 and 1956 was promising – it was he who not only started playing nasty modern music like *The Rite of Spring* but championed John Antill's *Corroboree*; as a composer, Goossens produced works like *The Apocalypse* – a bold and gargantuan vision of the end of the world as described in the Book of Revelation. As is well documented, Goossens' time in Australia ended in ignominy and scandal – he was busted by Customs at Sydney Airport with a case full of exotic masks and pornographic images. Regardless of his preferred private entertainments (after all, we have too much information about Percy Grainger and his whip collection), we can only speculate on how musical life in Sydney in particular would have developed had Goossens stayed on: it's one of the great might-have-beens in Australian musical life.

Margaret Sutherland divided her study between London and Vienna. In 1925 she returned to an Australia not quite ready for a musical language as 'advanced' as hers – though to our ears, her style is neo-classical rather than avant-garde. Her colleague Peggy Glanville-Hicks stayed away until the 1970s, returning only when her life's work as a composer was brought to a close by illness. Also returning to Australia in the early 1970s were Don Banks (1923–1980) and Keith Humble (1927–1995). Banks had first gone to London (where he and Sutherland formed the Australian Musical Association) and then on to Europe where he had studied with the doyen of American serialists, Milton Babbitt, and two of the most important figures in European music of their generation, Luigi Dallapiccola and Luigi Nono. Banks was able to forge one of the most distinctive voices of his generation, melding his other great musical love – jazz – with the advanced techniques of his European mentors. Humble likewise made his European landfall in Britain but soon found his way to Paris where he studied composition with, and became assistant to, Schoenberg pupil René Leibowitz.

There were thus at least two generations of significant Australian-born composers who were in touch with musical developments in Europe and their ranks were swelled by composers who had come to Australia as refugees in the wake of World War II and the fall of the Iron Curtain. Felix Werder arrived in Australia in 1940 after fleeing Nazi Germany with his family in 1935 and George Dreyfus escaped, also from Berlin, with his family in 1939. Both settled in Melbourne and have made that city the basis for their subsequent careers. Born to Russian Jewish parents in Tianjin, China, Larry Sitsky and his family came to Australia in 1951 after the victory of the Communist Party under Mao. This is not to suggest that these composers somehow carried with them the mystical bloodlines of contemporary European music; the point is that their cultural heritage made them more likely to be curious about such developments, without the deep-seated suspicion of things foreign that the Anglophone often displays. Werder, for instance, was far more au fait with atonality and the later twelve-note serial method of Schoenberg and his disciples. Banks and Humble trained in this method of composition in Europe; Werder was one of the few exploring its possibilities here. And Larry Sitsky remembers sitting down with Richard Meale to listen – for the first time for either of them – to a newly imported recording of Schoenberg's *Pierrot lunaire*. Sitsky 'couldn't get the sounds out of [his] head'.[1]

But the real problem was getting those sounds, and others like them, into the heads of the concert-going public. Bear in mind that the Australian premiere of Stravinsky's *The Rite of Spring* was in 1946 (that's 33 years after its first performance in Paris). The various kinds of European modernism, be they twelve-note serialism or wrong-note neo-classicism, were all being superseded in Europe by the time they made it to Australia. Not that there hadn't been attempts to raise consciousness beforehand: pianist/composer Roy Agnew produced a series of radio programs for the ABC as far back as 1937 (and lasting until 1942) in which he introduced listeners (those at least who didn't switch off and write outraged letters to the Commission's management) to the music of Schoenberg, Bartók, Honegger and other degenerates. But it fell to composers like Richard Meale and Nigel Butterley to modernise music broadcasting in the 1960s, and to Werder, Sitsky and Humble to found ensembles such as Australia Felix and the Australian Contemporary Music Ensemble for the live performance of new or unfamiliar work.

Covell's book provided a kind of snapshot of music in the late 1960s; in 1972 the indefatigable James Murdoch produced his *Australia's Contemporary Composers*; five years later the collection of essays edited by Frank Callaway and David Tunley, *Australian Composition in the Twentieth Century*, appeared. Inevitably a few of the composers have slipped off the radar, and indeed Margaret Seares, in her final summary chapter of the latter book, sensibly acknowledges the dangers of predicting the longevity or not of any given artist or work. But what is striking is how many of them were involved in advocacy and education: in addition to the formation of ensembles like ACME, these composers took academic positions at established institutions (Sculthorpe in Sydney, Meale in Adelaide, Colin Brumby in Brisbane) or helped to found new schools (Sitsky at the Canberra School of Music, ANU, and Humble at Melbourne's La Trobe). Callaway created a vibrant music department at the University of Western Australia that attracted composers of the calibre of Roger Smalley.

The 1970s saw exponential growth in music education, performance, broadcasting and composition. An important and influential figure who appears in the landscape in 1975 is the British musicologist Richard Toop, who took up a teaching position at the Sydney Conservatorium in that year. Toop brought with him first-hand experience of the post-war European avant-garde, having been an assistant teacher to Stockhausen in Cologne in the years before coming to Australia; one of his most recent writings is an excellent biography of the late György Ligeti. Toop's enthusiasm for European modernism was communicated to a group of students who emerged as important composers in the 1980s: Gerard Brophy (born 1953), Michael Smetanin (born 1958), Riccardo Formosa (born 1954) and Elena Kats-Chernin among them. Brophy came to musical study relatively late, and as an incipient guitarist attended masterclasses in 1976 with Brazilian virtuoso Turibio Santos and in 1977 with the puckish Argentinean composer Mauricio Kagel in Basle. Brophy returned to Sydney, and studied with Toop at the Sydney Conservatorium, later taking up an Australia Council Composer Fellowship which enabled him to study with Franco Donatoni at the Accademia Chigiana in Siena.

Donatoni (1927–2000), who also taught Australians Riccardo Formosa and Kati Tiutiunnik, took the constructivist preoccupations of the European avant-garde in a unique direction. Composers of the previous generation like Pierre Boulez and Stockhausen had sought, in their different ways, to expand the implications of Anton Webern's serialism. Webern, a student of Schoenberg's, had taken up his teacher's method of arranging the twelve notes of the chromatic scale into a row. Put simply: each note in the row must be sounded somewhere in the texture either as melody or part of a chord or counterpoint before any note can be repeated. The row can be subjected to various permutations (it can be used in retrograde, or inversion) but the principle remains the same. In his late works Webern seemed to be searching for a way of extending the principle into other parameters, but it was Boulez, in particular, who realised that parameters other than pitch could be serialised: not only could the notes of the chromatic scale be arranged in a fixed row but the composer could also predetermine a pattern of durations, dynamic and attacks. This is known as *integral serialism*. Donatoni saw that these processes were technically infinite and not inherently teleological. In his own work he used a number of automatic processes – what David Osmond-Smith writing in the *New Grove Dictionary* calls 'spontaneously chosen rules of substitution [and] elimination'.[2] In other words, one could, as Donatoni did, take a small fragment of an extant work and play any number of games with any given parameter – the possibilities were limitless, and in many ways it removed any vestige of the composer's personality from the work.

Or that was the theory, and for a time many Italian and foreign students of Donatoni's produced work that sounded pretty much alike – tempos were (or seemed) generally fast, foreground textures busy, thematic gestures bold. But Brophy's musical personality has always been a strong one and the 1980s saw the composition of many highly individual works: Flaubert's lurid novel *Salammbô* provided the inspiration for the eponymous *Salammbô* and *Mâtho*, both for large orchestra; *Lace* for string quartet and *Orfeo* for string orchestra are both rigorous and vibrantly energetic works. In 1988 Brophy composed *Forbidden Colours* (after the novel of the same name by Yukio Mishima) for small orchestra and, perhaps for the first time in his post-Donatonian phase, created a work in relatively slow tempo with shamelessly beautiful, subtle timbres and melodic fragments. Mishima's novel is set in the gay subculture of 1950s Tokyo; here one suspects the 'forbidden colours' are in fact musical elements eschewed by certain sections of the avant-garde. While Brophy continued to contribute to the subgenre of works with suggestive monosyllables for titles (*Flesh*, *Head*, *Glint*, *Tweak* and so on, no doubt taking a cue from Donatoni's *Blow* for wind quintet) his work moved, in pieces like *Forbidden Colours* and the larger-orchestral *Colour red … your mouth … heart* of 1994 to a more frankly sensual style often overlaid with Latin American elements.

Another student of Toop and later Donatoni was Riccardo Formosa who came to art music after a stellar career as lead guitarist and arranger with the Little River Band in the mid-1970s. Formosa's career in art music composition sadly, and bafflingly, lasted only a decade or so, during which he composed a small number of painstakingly crafted works. *Vertigo* for flute (doubling piccolo), oboe, clarinet and piano lives up to its title; *Dedica* for oboe and orchestra is a nine-minute master-piece, establishing a mosaic of hocketting textures and extravagantly florid solo writing, before a second section of long, wide-leaping but plangent oboe lines against icily beautiful orchestral sounds. Of this particular generation of Toop students Smetanin is perhaps the only one who has kept the modernist faith, though younger composers such as Damien Ricketson (born 1973), David Young and Anthony Pateras (born 1979) continue to explore the more speculative aspects of late modernism. Kats-Chernin, who after her time at the Sydney Conserv-atorium studied with Helmut Lachenmann in Germany, returned to Australia where she has progressively cultivated a style which admits elements of popular music – occasionally recalling cabaret or klezmer, fragments of standard repertoire, and mixture of Russian melancholy and cartoonish humour.

Smetanin's uncompromising style is not drily purist, and never was. In addition to the exposure to Stockhausen and Xenakis that Toop's tuition encouraged, and the particularly Dutch take on minimalism that he absorbed while studying with Louis Andriessen, Smetanin is also an old rocker – this can be heard clearly in the work that made his name in Europe, *Ladder of Escape*, and pieces with giveaway titles like *Hot Block*. Smetanin offered his fair share of suggestive monosyllables in *Spray*, *Strip* and *Stroke* and enjoyed the cause célèbre of his *Black Snow* (1988) being cancelled by one orchestra and nearly given the lid by a second. There is rather less self-conscious aggression in more recent works, though there is a high degree of stylistic continuity (and quality); his piano concerto *Mysterium cosmographicum* has a lapidary beauty, as does the recent ensemble work *Micrographia* though the latter also contains seriously funky passages, as in its long marimba solo.

Modernist Europhile sensibility was cultivated in various schools across the country. Keith Humble, as we've noted, taught at both the University of Melbourne and then at La Trobe, where he encouraged experimental, speculative composition (including the development of electronic music) with students and colleagues like Haydn Reeder (born 1944), Lawrence Whiffin (born 1930) and Jeff Pressing (1947–2002). Liza Lim studied in Melbourne with Riccardo Formosa, English composer turned motivational futurologist Richard Hames and then in the Netherlands with Ton de Leeuw; fellow Melburnian Mary Finsterer (born 1962), like Smetanin, studied in Amsterdam with Louis Andriessen. In Brisbane Stephen Cronin (born 1960) writes an intricate and complex music in a variety of genres, including ensemble pieces for Brisbane's Perihelion, the Seymour Group, Synergy, Duo Contemporain and Zurich's Octomania Ensemble.

Cronin's orchestral works include a powerful Piano Concerto and the even more shattering *Cries and Whispers* (1993). The latter takes its title only indirectly from the film of the same name by Ingmar Bergman; the composer was reading Bergman's autobiography *The Magic Lantern* at the time of the death of a close and much-admired friend. The piece 'would be a kind of celebration of my heroes, people whom I admired and perceived as role models'.[3] Among those are composers Gerard Brophy and Brian Howard. The affinities with those composers are strong, particularly the elaboration of texture through extravagant use of grace notes in polyphonic sections, creating a febrile texture, and the use of sforzando/crescendo patterns in the brass to establish harmonic supports. This twelve-minute piece begins, loudly, with three piccolos and the clarinet section at the top of their range playing a tangle of semitonal figures, to which a trio of trumpets adds emphatic commentary. This almost hysterical background, which recurs as a kind of ritornello, persists as other sections of the orchestra weigh in with dense string chords and high horn calls. The contrasting 'whispers' section which follows is based on multiple divided upper strings in a complex web of soft sound, with glints provided by woodwinds playing a kind of hocket (each instrument plays isolated single notes at different times). The central section of the work has a downward trajectory: trilling winds against string figures which use ever slower moving groupings, creating a sense of exhaustion. While the overall impression of the work is strident, there are passages of extreme tenderness for two solo violins, and after a frenetic outburst from the full orchestra, a section for harp, divided cellos and double bass. It can't last though, and a version of the earlier hysteria returns, building to fever pitch with the addition of an air-raid siren that wails like some Titan in pain. The piece's end is loud and brutal, a forceful chord which slips downwards into nothingness.

Melburnian composer David Chisholm (born 1970) recently presented what he calls an 'epic song cycle', *The Beginning and the End of Snow*, for soprano, clarinet, keyboard (harpsichord, piano and celesta), harp, viola and cello to poetry by French writer Yves Bonnefoy. Such a combination is richly suited to the atmospherics of Bonnefoy's verse, be it in the shivering of the harpsichord writing, the spangles from the celesta or even the jazzish piano when the poet contemplates the return of summer. Warmth is provided, where necessary, by the low strings and clarinet (doubling bass), and the vocal lines are generous and sensual – the sort of music Debussy might have written 100 years on.

Georges Lentz, mentioned in 'Going native?', casts his extraordinary meditations in a richly textured musical fabric. Brett Dean (born 1961), like Lentz, enjoys a career evenly divided between Australia and Europe and is completely undogmatic about style, but uses the expressive possibilities of late modernist style to underpin deeply held humanist concerns.

Brett Dean: Music as Memorial

Most composers start pretty early, eventually, as Richard Toop once remarked, producing their first fully individual works in their late twenties, but Brett Dean breaks that mould. In 1984 he went to Germany where he played viola in the Berlin Philharmonic for some 15 years. He only began actively composing (in his late twenties) towards the end of that decade, and indeed regards the clarinet concerto *Ariel's Music*, which he wrote for his brother Paul Dean in 1995, as his first mature work. The title refers not to Shakespeare's airy spirit in *The Tempest* or the name occasionally given to Jerusalem in the Bible, but to a young American girl who died of AIDS in 1988, and whose mother – who had contracted the disease through a blood transfusion – became a heroic campaigner for the cause in a country which had experienced denial at the highest levels of government.

This in itself sets part of the agenda for much of Dean's prolific output since. His music is politically and ethically outspoken; as such it is very much a part of the historic role of the post-war European avant-garde, especially in Germany where Dean lived for so long. This is not to say that Dean is a doctrinaire modernist, complexifist or whatever else. His music is, broadly speaking, post-diatonic in idiom, not afraid to make aggressive or discomforting sounds, but these are always in the service of a humanistic approach to his work; he is equally at ease in serene 'tonal' regions where they might be appropriate to what he wishes to express. *Ariel's Music* is a work with a cause and the same might be said for several of Dean's subsequent pieces. In 2001, for instance, he composed the orchestral fanfare *Dispersal*, the implications of whose title range, as Dean puts it:

> from the transitive 'scattering widely in different directions' to the intransitive 'leave-taking to go in different ways', or from even more specific scientific terms, such as 'distributing small particles in a medium' (chemistry) to 'dividing white light into its coloured constituents' (physics). 'Dispersal', in colonial Australian parlance, was a widely used euphemism for the pursuit and mass slaughter of Aborigines.[4]

Dispersal was written a year after Dean returned to Australia, settling on Queensland's Sunshine Coast at first – the inspiration for his 2001 *Pastoral Symphony* – and then in Melbourne. *Pastoral Symphony* is one of several works in which Dean simultaneously celebrates the natural world and mourns its degradation. Appalled by the 2002 Bali bombing and the Iraq War in 2003, Dean found himself drawn into one of the many Melbourne churches that had opened their doors for private prayer for peace on behalf of the civilians and military personnel caught in those conflicts. The result of this was another orchestral work, *Ceremonial*, a 'space for thought and prayer'. A few years before, in 1999, Dean produced the major orchestral work *Beggars and Angels* inspired by an exhibition of angel paintings by his partner Heather Betts and sculptures of beggars by Trak Wendisch. Using some material from a solo viola piece, *Intimate Decisions*, Dean composed a huge musical canvas of immense dramatic contrasts and emotional ambiguity. The work, moreover, includes another memorial: a tuba solo, marked 'For Frank' remembers Frank Barzyk, an Australian tuba player who died tragically young. Barzyk was, incidentally, the player for whom Dean's colleague Brenton Broadstock wrote an ecstatically beautiful concerto in 1985.

Dean's orchestral music has, among other things, an amazing technical proficiency. As a violist he, like many composers before him such as Mozart, Beethoven, Dvoák and Britten, literally has an inside view of how such music works. It also means Dean's ability to write solo and chamber music, especially that founded on string combinations, has great formal poise. *Intimate Decisions* is a tour de force for solo viola using the full gamut of sounds of which the instrument is normally capable; in the first version of *Testament*, for 12 violas, he goes one step further. That work is based on Dean's response to Beethoven's 'Heiligenstadt Testament'. In 1802 Beethoven wrote a kind of will addressed (but never sent) to his two brothers explaining how the realisation of impending deafness had led him to contemplate suicide until his sense of mission as an artist persuaded him to keep going. It was only discovered among Beethoven's papers after his death, so its significance is in the way it represents a kind of exorcism. Dean creates a powerful and at times terrifying musical image of Beethoven's state of mind at the time. He does this in part by directing the players at various times to use an un-rosined bow with the result that it gives an inchoate, toneless

Brett Dean: *Testament*, pp. 14–15 showing the quotations from Beethoven threaded through the texture. ©2003 by Boosey and Hawkes, Bote and Bock, Berlin. Reprinted by kind permission.

sound, perhaps representing Beethoven's frantically writing down what is in his teeming brain as well as an image of what it might be like to be unable to hear; Dean describes it as a music of 'almost silent desperation'. (See music example.) As the piece progresses, chunks of the first movement of Beethoven's first 'Razumovsky' Quartet (Op. 59 No. 1) gradually appear; later in the piece, after an impassioned outburst for the full band (all using rosined bows), short quotations of Beethoven's finale can be heard. (The 'Razumovsky' Quartets are the first examples of Beethoven's 'heroic' style in this genre: the first can be compared to the *Eroica* Symphony in the way it burst the bounds of conventional scale and expression, and on the score of the third, Beethoven famously wrote, 'Let your deafness no longer be secret, even in art.')

Dean's empathy with Beethoven's distress is of a piece with his memorialisation of people dead before their time. His use of quotation, as in *Testament*, also forges links between his personal style and various aspects of the western tradition. In *Dispersal* he quotes a hymn tune often sung to the words 'O Brother Man, Fold to thy Heart thy Brother', the irony of course being that the ideals of the hymn's abolitionist poet, John Greenleaf Whittier, are as unfulfilled now as when he wrote those words. Quotation also functions to evoke 'aspects of memory, and to some extent about the somewhat misleading and fickle nature of memory, the tricks that it can play on you; making things worse or better, rosier or bleaker than they in fact were at the time', as he writes in his note to the recent chamber piece *Recollections*, which quotes a short *Romanze* by Clara Schumann.

One of Dean's finest chamber works is his *Huntington Eulogy*, which, like Tennyson's poem *In Memoriam*, transcends grief by seeing it in a cosmic context. In that respect it brings together two of the preoccupations we have noted in Dean's work: remembering the dead and celebrating the natural world.

Brett Dean conducting. Photo by Bridget Elliot.

The first two movements of *Huntington Eulogy* celebrate the beauty of the Mudgee region; the third, which relates thematically to its predecessors, is an elegy for a young winemaker from the area, Jason Brodie. The first movement, 'Nightsky', evokes, in the composer's words, 'a spacious dark sense of mystery and awe'. The pianist produces unusual timbres by plucking and, with a soft timpani stick, tapping the strings, as the cello spins out a long phrase whose expressive nature is enhanced by the use of microtonal intervals (like 'note bending' in jazz singing). A series of shorter phrases lead to a long and ecstatic melody very high in the cello's range, accompanied by gently undulating figurations from the piano, before the opening gesture returns, now interrupted by terse motifs from the piano and a shivering 'nervous' figure from the cello.

'Swarming' evokes a swarm of bees which, one summer morning, put a slightly different complexion on the composer's quiet communing with nature. These are serious bees, beginning loudly in the bass regions of the piano with a frenetic *moto perpetuo* offset by rapid changes of metre and accent. The cello buzzes and trills and uses the white-noise timbre of *sul ponticello*, though there are passages of 'unexpected eerie sweetness' and the limpid sound of natural harmonics.

The piano begins the final 'Elegy' with a reminiscence of the cello's opening gesture – necessarily free of microtonal inflexions. A short motif and long held harmonic from the cello announce a variant of the high melody from 'Nightsky', now in the register of a human voice and, at first, even more simply diatonic. The melody tends inevitably downward, and the movement ends with a delicate tracery of piano writing against the spectral sound of double-stopped harmonics on the cello.

While much of Dean's work deals with grief and anxiety, it is shot through with beautiful sound, and as Maynard Solomon remarks in his biography of Mozart:

> Beauty heals, comforts, transforms, preserves, remembers promises, buries the dead and raises them up again, reminds us not only of what we have lost but of what may be ours again, if only as a symbol.[5]

Damien Ricketson: What Miles of Diamonds

In 1990 Roger Woodward founded the Sydney Spring International Festival of New Music, which ran for twelve years. It was a festival devoted to presenting works and performers from the pointy end of new music, with generous offerings of the music of Iannis Xenakis, James Dillon, Horatiu Radulescu and Rolf Gelhaar – to name some of the international composers featured. Through the festival Woodward also continued to support Australian composers: those like Sculthorpe and Boyd with whom he had a long association, established composers of more recent generations and those at the start of their careers. The festival was also responsible for the formation of at least two new ensembles that went on to have lives of their own. The Alpha Centauri Ensemble, later renamed Sydney Alpha, went on to present a distinguished series of concerts in its own right but has sadly since been disbanded. Still going, though, is Ensemble Offspring, initially formed to play at the Festival. One of its founders, Damien Ricketson, was one of the younger composers for whom Sydney Spring was an important launching pad.

Ricketson studied first at the Sydney Conservatorium and then with Louis Andriessen in The Hague as well as at IRCAM in Paris. Since his return to Sydney he has taught at the Conservatorium and remains artistic director of Ensemble Offspring. As we might expect from a composer who has passed through the orbits of both Andriessen and Boulez, Ricketson's music is late-modernist in aesthetic, experimental in form and speculative in content. It's also very beautiful.

His early work, *Ptolemy's Onion*, premiered at the Sydney Spring Festival in 1998 and demonstrates a number of features of Ricketson's work. Scored for bass flute and string quartet – all instruments are amplified, but the ensemble should be placed as far from the audience as possible – the work lasts around 20 minutes and falls into seven linked sections. The title refers to the astronomical system proposed by Ptolemy in second century Alexandria. A series of concentric circles with the earth at its centre represents the interlocking orbits of heavenly bodies. Ricketson's metaphor of the onion is at once a simple visual analogue to the Ptolemaic system and a description of the layering process that underpins his composition. The work's pitch content is generated in the first instance from eight simple 'root melodies'. These are never stated literally but are 'filtered' in various ways by what the composer describes as 'oscillating', 'frenzied' and 'timeless' environments; the environments dictate the character of any given passage, as well as how the root melody's pitch material is dispersed throughout the ensemble. There are further 'epicycles', patterns that determine other aspects of the work: one moves between pure and 'noisy' tone-production, another between relative degrees of consonance and dissonance and a third between degrees of homogeneity and heterogeneity within the ensemble. These cycles have their own independent periods ensuring the music's sense of constant – even if on occasion very slow – change. As Ricketson notes, the musical material is in some respects:

> embellished to an almost ridiculous level with complex rhythmic articulations, grace notes, trills, pitch-bends, flutter-tongue (flute),

jeté, harmonics and double-stops (strings): an ornamental music that is indulging in its own virtuosic excess. At the same time, and at another level, the shadow of the same melody is stated in its most essential and unadorned form: artificial harmonics in the case of the strings and 'ghost tones' in the case of the flute.[6]

In other words, the music gives a sense of the 'majestic clockwork', but the complexity and independence of the structuring layers and principles mean that the work in no way sounds like it's going through the motions. And it contains some exquisite sounds. For instance, the bass flute begins the work, in rhythmic unison with the first violin (some octaves higher), with a relatively simple melody inflected by overblown harmonics (thus slightly out of tune to the equal-tempered ear). Contrasting with this is the cold interstellar sounds of string harmonics, emphatic rhythmic iterations and expressive melodies (especially for cello) where the use of microtonal inflection might suggest the shakuhachi or erhu. Perhaps aware of Sir Francis Bacon's often-quoted remark that 'there is no excellent beauty that hath not some strangeness in the proportion', Ricketson smartly offsets his cosmic vision with an all-too-human epilogue, called 'I Wheeze' where the flautist moves away from the ensemble and starts playing a childlike solo on the recorder.

Ricketson's interest in eternal processes is evident in several works, notably *Porphyrius' Shuffle* for solo piano, in which the musical material and expressive instructions are presented as two separate 'loops': the pianist must decide at which point in each 'loop' to begin playing, ensuring that no two performances will be identical. This flexibility carries over into what Ricketson calls 'open-score' works like *Trace Elements*, which can be played by any two wind and any two string instruments. The score is written in tablature rather than pitched notation: the wind instruments are given graphically precise fingerings, though the pitch produced by, say, the first and second finger of the left hand will vary wildly from, say, flute to contrabassoon; the string writing likewise concentrates on finger position and the production of natural harmonics. (See music example.) Ricketson thus prefers to use two different instruments from each family. Failing that, if there are, for instance, two violins available, the composer requests that one be retuned to broaden the available pitches. But there will always be certain relationships that are constant – the contour if not the pitch content of the melodic writing, for instance; every performance will be different, but will be recognisably the same piece. The use of tablature was inspired by a sixteenth-century manuscript, the Crakow Lute Tablature, which for Ricketson gave the piece a link to its commissioning body, the Warsaw Autumn Festival. The idea of ancient or lost musics is an abiding interest of Ricketson's.

In *A Line Has Two* Ricketson has explored the notion of openness and the concept of time passing – both crucial aspects of works we have already mentioned – through a collaboration with the distinguished Australian poet Christopher Wallace-Crabbe. An amalgam of the extant

Damien Ricketson: *Trace Elements*, page 28. This 'open score' is notated in tablature, giving fingering patterns rather than absolute pitch. Used by permission of the composer.

poem *The Alignments* and material written especially for this piece, Wallace-Crabbe's text is an extended meditation on time and change, full of striking, spacious imagery like that of the impassive ocean's 'miles of diamonds'. This substantial piece further demonstrates the composer's love of the archaic by the inclusion of the ancient double-reed *aulos* in the ensemble. The score also calls for soprano, two clarinets, two percussionists and pre-recorded electronics, and the percussion rig includes 12 differently tuned wine glasses arranged geometrically and designated *tusut* after an ancient middle-eastern instrument.

Ricketson, with the poet's agreement, has not simply set Wallace-Crabbe's verse. The text is 'delivered' in three forms: written (the printed program), spoken (pre-recorded) and sung. And in keeping with his interest in open forms and endless recombinations, Ricketson has treated the text as so many movable modules. The musical and textual information, then, comes to us in hints and fragments, though the formal shape of the work is more than satisfying, even containing a climax of traditional 'singerly' writing towards the end. It also breaks new ground, for Ricketson, in its use of direct quotation from other music. The work is about time passing, 'valediction and renewal', so Ricketson quotes from two sources: the final 'Ewig ...' ('eternally') motif from the last movement of Mahler's *Das Lied von der Erde* to symbolise valediction, and, for renewal, the 'Song of the Unborn Children' from Richard Strauss' *Die Frau ohne Schatten*. (The Strauss also connects with the glass *tusut*, as the glass harmonica features in the opera.) The appearances of the Mahler tend to be immediately recognisable; the Strauss tune, however, is put through the sorts of distorting filters we met in *Ptolemy's Onion*, generating a lot of new, distantly related material.

Ricketson has said that 'in the noisy world of public utterances, I am more attentive to private sounds'. His refined and detailed work gives the impression of seeing a world in a grain of sand.

Chapter 8

The Tyranny of Dissonance?

Twelve-tone music is like a building without windows or doors.

Peggy Glanville-Hicks[1]

It all got pretty ugly around 1990. Not music, that is, but the discussion of it in Australia – or at least in *Sounds Australian*, then the official journal of the Australian Music Centre. What it boiled down to was a simplistic and often acrimonious disagreement about style. In the red corner, there were the proponents of an uncompromising modernist aesthetic in which one could faintly discern the remains of the avant-garde's political program. To backtrack briefly: for a young artist in late 1940s and early 1950s Europe it must have been tempting to want to clear the deck completely. The Nazis had remained devotees of the music of Beethoven and Wagner even as they had systematically murdered millions of innocent people. Culture was seen to be complicit in crime, so artists and philosophers argued that art, if it could exist after Auschwitz, needed to start with a complete carte blanche, free of any reference back to the tainted culture which preceded the war. Art needed to unmask any kind of optimism as false consciousness. Moreover, many artists held that history itself would dictate the one and only way forward in the development of their art form: essentially in a kind of Marxist-Darwinist way, this would involve ever greater levels of formal complexity.

As the twentieth century wore on, the political aspect of the avant-garde assumed less urgency. In Europe, for instance, Pierre Boulez dropped his 'blow up the opera houses' rhetoric in favour of a comb-over and gigs conducting Wagner, while continuing to add to his small but exquisite oeuvre. But the sense of the artist as a solitary figure, misunderstood by the population at large (but frequently drawing a university salary), continued to hold some Romantic appeal for some composers. Even Larry Sitsky, in his recent and valuable study of Australian piano music[2], reprints (with a commentary) an article he wrote outlining his Manichean view: there are 'composers' and 'anti-composers'. The former write longer, faster and technically more complex works, and cling to a Romantic-modernist notion of the 'difficulty' of both the art and the artist; the latter write short, slow, simple works, and get their pictures in the newspaper.

On the other hand, the 1970s saw a number of significant Australian composers experience a Damascene road conversion from modernism to a renewed interest in diatonic music. For Colin Brumby (born 1933), the realisation that he couldn't hear an egregious mistake in a performance of one of his own works made him reaffirm tonality in 1974 'as the means by which I can articulate form with most conviction'[3]; for Richard Meale it was the growing suspicion that 'feelings of affection, of love and tenderness – did not seem to me to be accessible in such a complicated style of writing'.[4] Meale's change of style can be seen in works like the orchestral *Viridian* of 1979 – a work of shamelessly frank Debussyism – and the String Quartet No. 2, written in memory of his best friend. Of the next generation, Ross Edwards felt, in the early 1970s, that the avant-garde style he had cultivated was 'very neurotic'; his subsequent conversion to the spare, contemplative manner of his so-called 'sacred style', and the ebullience of the *maninya* style which appeared soon after, have laid the foundations for his mature output.

Of course the rediscovery of tonality was nothing of the sort, and certainly not a case of psychological regression peculiar to Australian composers. The Stravinskys and Brittens of this world had continued to make diatonic harmony the basis of their musical language from the 1930s; the exploration of non-European traditions that we've discussed in relation to Sculthorpe and his protégés had its parallels in other parts of the world. And the rise of such styles as minimalism in the United States affirmed the centrality of the common chord. But around 1990 the resurgence of tonality among younger composers in Australia led to an unedifying series of exchanges in the pages of the Australian Music Centre journal, where 'maximalists' and a shadowy group called the Adelaide Pastoral Company traded insults. This all generated much more heat than light and, the laws of thermodynamics being what they are, it ultimately ran out of energy; Australian composition now enjoys a state of détente or comfortable plurality, if not of mutual respect.

Graeme Koehne (born 1956) is one of the most voluble anti-modernists among Australian composers. In the 1990s he devoted considerable energy to a series of orchestral works that aspire to the condition of pop music. The cultivation of a pop sensibility is perhaps the closest a composer in as highly urbanised a society as Australia can get to folk music. Nigel Westlake (born 1958) blazed this particular trail as a young composer in the 1970s when he formed a 'classical/jazz-rock/world-music fusion band' before further study in the Netherlands. Much of Westlake's subsequent compositional career has been in film music (*Babe*, *Miss Potter*), but he has produced a significant body of concert music beginning with the percussion quartet *Omphalo Centric Lecture*. Something of a classic, this work takes its title from a painting by Paul Klee, but stylistically derives from African *balofon* (or xylophone) music. Overall Westlake's music tends to cultivate deceptively simple tonal harmony and often minimalist rhythmic figures to create a sense of great energy. He is also capable of music of crystalline elegance, like the chamber work *Refractions at Summercloud Bay* as well as breathtaking virtuosity in his *Oscillations* for piano duo. Matthew Hindson (born 1968) has cultivated a grittier kind of pop in techno-inspired works like *Homage to Metallica, Headbanger* and *Death stench* as he is drawn to what he has described as the 'unpretentious' nature of such music. This is mirrored in a number of works that celebrate contemporary life (*Speed, Rush, Nintendo music*) whose concerns come together in the four-movement *Symphony of Modern Objects*.

And the symphony has made a comeback principally in the music of those composers who now embrace diatonicism. This is not surprising: the tonal system is at heart goal-directed. It establishes a home key, and creates drama by teasing, subverting and finally fulfilling the listener's expectations of how and when that 'homecoming' will be effected; that's how Mozart creates the extraordinary build-up of tension over large spans of time in, say, the finales to *The Marriage of Figaro*. Modern symphonies don't, of course, feel the need to adopt sonata form or other classical manners, but they do, broadly speaking, need to create the sense of an ongoing argument and a drama born of harmonic and rhythmic contrast. To generalise, musical languages where the push and pull of dissonance and consonance is eradicated – be it by the total dissonance of serialism or the repetition of patterns in minimalism – tend to create works which exist in the moment rather than the expectation of something yet to come. Stockhausen's concept of moment form reflects this, as does those works by Boulez or Conyngham where the musical elements can be freely assembled by the performer: they celebrate time's cycle rather than time's arrow.

Reports of the death of the symphony (like that of the orchestra itself) have been exaggerated, though in this country new orchestral works still tend to be the 10–12 minute curtain-raisers much favoured by the ABC and its now devolved clutch of orchestras. Alfred Hill, of course, had written a dozen or so symphonies, and a number of our senior composers (Roger Smalley, Richard Meale, Don Kay, Philip Braanin) have produced individual (or small numbers of) symphonies but it is Carl Vine (born 1954), Ross Edwards and Brenton Broadstock (born 1952) who have produced a substantial body of work in the genre. Vine's symphonies adhere closest to the spirit of the classical symphony, being mostly large-scale, abstract works driven by the dramatic possibilities of the tonal system. Brenton Broadstock, by comparison, is passionate about communicating ideas and emotions through his work. His beautifully crafted symphonies are full of the *lacrimae rerum*, the tears in all things, be it the process of coming to terms with having a disabled child, the experience of mental illness or an angel weeping at the miseries of human existence. Edwards is similarly concerned with a range of extra-musical concerns: a prayer for peace, an elegy for the earth or a hymn to the cosmos. There have also been a number of substantial symphonic poems, for want of a better term, in recent years: Barry Conyngham's *Now that darkness* (2004), Nigel Butterley's *From Sorrowing Earth*, Brett Dean's *Beggars and Angels* and Paul Stanhope's *Fantasia on a theme of Vaughan Williams* (2003) spring to mind, while as we have noted, Georges Lentz's ongoing exploration of the mysteries of the universe in sound and silence continues to bear important fruit in several large-scale works of his *Mysterium* series.

Graeme Koehne: That's Entertainment

Graeme Koehne studied with Richard Meale in Adelaide at a time when the older composer was re-evaluating his own commitment to the virtues of musical modernism. You will remember that when Meale came to write his String Quartet No. 2 he wanted to cultivate simplicity as a means of directly communicating human feelings of 'affection, love and tenderness' which, he had come to feel, was not possible in the

complicated language of modernist music. So, despite dutifully absorb-
ing the lessons of post-Webernian music, in 1982 Koehne produced
the orchestral work *Rain forest*, which staked an unequivocal claim to
the territory that he would subsequently explore. That work, which
won the Australian Composers Award at the 1982 Adelaide Festival
and was ranked third at the Paris International Rostrum of Composers
the same year, was, like Meale's *Viridian* of 1979, unapologetically
post-impressionist in a way reminiscent of Takemitsu. The award of a
Harkness Fellowship in 1984 enabled Koehne to travel to the United
States. There he studied at Yale University with Louis Andriessen, but
more influential was his private study with Virgil Thomson. Thomson's
views about the primacy of melody clearly had a strong bearing on such
works as Koehne's neo-Mozartian Capriccio for Piano and Strings of
1987.

Koehne's embrace of diatonicism and what he describes as 'traditional classical process'[5] have made his music eminently suited to ballet.
The Selfish Giant written in 1982 for the Sydney Dance Company
established his reputation as a composer for dance. Since then he has
composed *Gallery* for the Australian Ballet (1987), *Once around the
Sun* for the Queensland Ballet (1988) and, for the Australian Ballet
in 1997, *1914*, which takes its scenario from David Malouf's novel set
during World War I, *Fly away Peter*, and is full of strongly terpsichorean
rhythms and melodic ostinatos, and satisfyingly constructed dramatic
sections. In 2005 he composed *Tivoli* for the Sydney Dance Company.
Other works for the stage include the chamber opera *Love Burns* (1992)
and an opera for children, *Grandma's Shoes* (2000). He has also written music for the classic 1927 Australian silent film, *The Kid Stakes*
(1994).

The 1990s also saw the series of orchestral works with clearly popu-
list intent: *Powerhouse* is a rhumba for orchestra which pays homage to
the music of Warner Bros' genius cartoon composer Carl Stalling and
to Raymond Scott, whose 'Powerhouse' was used by Stalling to depict
machinery and bulldogs; *Unchained melody* refers to the music of Stevie
Wonder, and Koehne's Oboe Concerto for Diana Doherty is entitled

Inflight Entertainment. Of the latter work, Koehne writes:

> 'Entertainment' is also one of my favourite words. I particularly like to use it to see the shocking effect it has on many of my composer colleagues and newspaper critics. I've often heard it said that 'entertainment' is not a value that a contemporary composer should consider, but I think that music which does not set out to entertain ends up being boring. To entertain means to excite the senses and the imagination.[6]

He goes on to argue that:

> Even in some of the most standard of movie genres, there is inventive and innovative music which deserves to be admired and studied. In fact, there is often more skill, technique and imagination to be found in the work of these composers who were working for a commercial purpose, than in the inflated pretension of much 'contemporary classical' music.

Koehne is quick to acknowledge that the distinction between popular and classical music is blurred, and in this he is in good company. 'Classical' composers throughout history have realised how porous the boundary is: there is any number of medieval and renaissance works which mix the sacred and profane; Mozart took a predominantly ecclesiastical instrument – the trombone – into the opera theatre for heart-stopping moments in *Don Giovanni*; Beethoven used the noisy effects of French Revolutionary 'Rescue' Opera to shore up the massive structures of his *Eroica* Symphony. One could go on.

Sometimes Koehne's deliberately provocative rhetoric is so successful at annoying his critics that the deeper structural processes of his music are overlooked. In a work like *Elevator Music* (1997), for instance, we see the familiar gambit of a title which dares the 'elitist' musician to dismiss the work and, as Koehne puts it in his program note, 'register disdain for any kind of music which serves to give pleasure to "ordinary" people'. He goes on to note the influence of Les Baxter, Henry Mancini and John Barry, all of whom 'built upon their classical schooling to integrate jazz and popular music into orchestral music'. Barry, as Koehne points out, not only wrote music for many of the great *James Bond* movies but had been an important figure in British rock'n'roll in the 1950s.

So Koehne's piece is, of course, emphatically not the sort of thing anyone, ordinary or not, might care to hear in an elevator. It has a powerful and unremitting beat announced at the start by a percussion grouping that features timpani (in homage to the John Barry Seven's timpanist Dougie Wright) and sets up an ostinato of eight fast quavers where the fourth and fifth are tied. This generates tremendous momentum pushed on by interlocking figures in the lower woodwinds and a broad melody in the upper strings. The work's first climax introduces a new rhythmic ostinato of dotted crotchet-dotted crotchet-crotchet (123,123,12). This appears in four-bar groups outlining a repeated harmonic pattern of G major-F major with augmented fifth-G major-F minor 7. The two rhythmic patterns, used together and separately, provide the constant pulse of the work over its eight-minute span.

On the surface then, we have a piece of good-natured, energetic music – but it is not quite as simple as it seems. Those sinuously interlocking figures at the work's opening, which begin in the bass clarinet and move upward through clarinet, oboe and flute sections, are iterations of a six-note figure, and a highly chromatic one at that (A flat, B flat, A natural, D flat, E flat, G flat). The first countermelody (on horns, contrabassoon and double bass) uses the same pitches in a different order. So there is a saturation of six, more-or-less constantly circulating pitches for the first thirty bars, at which point we reach that first climax. There is, as I have said, a new rhythmic figure; in addition the harmony stresses the G major triad and an augmented triad using F and C sharp while the woodwind ostinatos reiterate the note E.

In other words, Koehne has systematically used all twelve notes of the chromatic scale, and these two hexachords – groups of six notes – provide much of the harmonic material of the whole piece. As the composer notes: 'I haven't used any of the conventional 12-tone meth-

Graeme Koehne: *Elevator Music*, bars 7–8 (bass clarinet only).

Graeme Koehne: *Elevator Music*, bars 31–34.

The bass clarinet outlines the six-note figure which dominates until bar 31, when the 'other' six notes are filled in. Used by permission of the composer.

ods of developing this material, though. That's where Messrs Baxter, Mancini and Barry come in ...' and wistfully remarks that it is 'a possibility I wish Schoenberg had thought of − one day while playing tennis with Gershwin, perhaps'.[7] To be fair, Schoenberg had discovered the dramatic possibilities of playing off hexachords as early as *Erwartung* in 1909, and continued to fashion harmony out of pairs of six-note chords where the second 'resolves' the first for the rest of his life. It's an old trick, but it works; that's entertainment.

Ross Edwards and the Love that Moves the Stars

In 1982 composer Ross Edwards was sitting on a bus trying to think of a way to describe his latest work, the Piano Concerto, for a program note. The task was more than usually difficult as Edwards had produced a work atypical of his own current style and defiantly at odds with modernist orthodoxy. After study with Richard Meale and Peter Sculthorpe in Sydney, and with Peter Maxwell Davies and Sandor Veress in Adelaide, Edwards, like many of his generation, travelled to the UK where he was forced to confront his relationship to the music of the European avant-garde. His deep feeling of alienation from that aesthetic led to a crisis in the early 1970s from which issued what some commentators describe as Edwards' 'sacred style'. Edwards explained to composer Andrew Ford that his work to that point had been 'very neurotic. And I wanted to calm down; I wanted to gradually find another language.'[8] Born of an immersion in eastern philosophy, notably Zen Buddhism, and the contemplation of environmental sounds in bushland near the New South Wales central coast town of Pearl Beach, Edwards' 'sacred' works, or as he better describes them, 'objects of musical contemplation', eschew traditional western processes of melody and harmony, development and elaboration, make intense use of silence and the hypnotic power of repetition, and create a sense of existing outside time.

But later in the 1970s Edwards had had another defining moment, this time a powerful experience of the joy of physical existence. The realisation that he had the 'privilege of living in a paradise of sun-blessed ocean and joyously shrieking parrots gyrating in the warm air' led Edwards to a new manner, known as his 'maninya' style (from a non-signifying text that he wrote for one of the early works of this type). Here the music is active, full of dance rhythms, happily using an open-hearted tonal or modal harmony, and the Piano Concerto was just such a piece. Sitting on the bus in 1982, Edwards wrote that the traditional simplicity of the work was 'an absolutely one-off, I'm never going to write a piece like this again'. Famous last words, as the Piano Concerto (though since extensively re-worked) laid the foundation for a rapprochement with the tradition of western music which has since borne fruit in a series of substantial orchestral works including five symphonies.

Edwards' Symphony No. 1, *Da Pacem Domine*, which was composed in 1991, has no vocal component but 'embraces the world', to borrow Mahler's phrase, through its references to a fragment of Gregorian chant. Two major events helped shape the work: the first Gulf Crisis which led to military intervention in Kuwait in January of that year; and the mortal illness of conductor Stuart Challender, Chief Conductor of the Sydney Symphony Orchestra and champion of new music, to whom the work is dedicated. In his own program note for the premiere performance (by the West Australian Symphony Orchestra under Jorge Mester) Edwards wrote:

> A large, monolithic single movement, the Symphony evolves slowly and organically over a deep, insistent rhythmic pulse. It is thus, in effect, a sort of massive orchestral chant of quiet intensity into which my subjective feelings of grief and foreboding about some of the great threats to humanity: war, pestilence and environmental devastation, have been subsumed into the broader context of ritual. And although it is manifestly more architectonic than some of my other 'contemplative' music, the Symphony is designed to create a sense of timelessness associated with certain Oriental and Mediaeval Western musical genres. A hymn-like episode based on a fragment of the plainsong *Da pacem Domine* (Give peace, Lord) gives the work its title.[9]

The work begins quietly, in the lower regions of the orchestra, with the insistent figure of a semitone rising and falling, as if struggling for expression. The orchestral texture very gradually gains increased mass, building to rich, fully scored statements of the material derived from the plainchant. The harmonic language of the work is simple and modal, occasionally recalling some of the more luminous textures of Vaughan Williams. As composer Paul Stanhope has noted, the Symphony is an example of 'sacred style' in its 'brooding and quiet nature' but its triadic harmony brings it closer to that of the 'maninya' pieces. For all its simplicity, however, the Symphony never quite slips the surly bonds of earth. Embodying the unsung chant, the fully scored tutti sections are satisfyingly climactic, but the piece as a whole, rather like the final pages of Britten's *War Requiem*, never quite achieves musical resolution. In fact the work has a kind of arch shape, ending, as it began, in the depths. As Edwards has said in an interview with ABC's Rachel Kohn, 'I tried to transcend all these dark feelings in the piece. And at moments I may have, but it sort of goes black at the end, and people get very upset by it.'[10] The symphony is a prayer for peace, not a description of peace having been achieved; we see the empty tomb, but, not yet at least, the risen Christ.

A decade later, Edwards completed his Symphony No. 4, *Star Chant*. In the interim he had produced his second, *Earth Spirit Song*, with texts for solo soprano by the medieval mystic Hildegard of Bingen and Australian poet Judith Wright. The landscapes celebrated in Wright's poetry are not comfortable, pastoral scenes, but as many commentators have noted, her work taught us to see the landscape for what it was, not for how it might ideally be. Wright frequently deplores the damage wrought by European-style farming – and makes no secret that her 'squattocrat' forebears have much for which to answer; but her evocations of 'pristine' landscapes can nonetheless be tinged with menace. 'The Lost Man', from the 1953 collection *The Gateway*, which Edwards features in his Second Symphony, is a case in point. As Edwards has noted, in 'the mystical depths of Judith Wright's rainforest ... euphoria evaporates and we are confronted by primeval forces that would efface the psyche and absorb it into the eternal cycles of nature'.[11] Significantly, Wright overlays the imagery of the rainforest with subtle Christological symbols: the lost man has had a painful journey, with bleeding hands and feet, and may at the end have been redeemed through water. This symphony, like much of Edwards' most recent music, ranges freely between the ancient musical heritage of Christian liturgy and his own 'singing' of various Australian landscapes.

His Third Symphony, *Mater Magna*, is a 'meditation on the need for ecological re-balancing'. Again the songs and sounds of the natural world – birds, insects and frogs – provide a vibrant musical language laced with fragmentary references to a Gregorian chant associated with the Hail Mary (*Ave Maria gratia plena*), thus identifying the Virgin with the mythological Great Mother; the work finally issues in the melody, *Dawn Mantras*, that Edwards wrote for the 2000 Millennium celebrations, rung out on wild bells cast to celebrate the centenary of Australia's federation.[12]

It seems almost inevitable, then, that having essayed the pessimistic world-view of *Da Pacem Domine*, and our relationship to the physical world in the subsequent two works, Edwards should turn his attention to the wider cosmos as he does in Symphony No. 4, *Star Chant*. The composer has noted that:

> to William Blake, the stars were coldly and logically Satanic. To the Australian Aboriginal peoples they have been familiar, meaningful and ultimately benevolent. And indeed, to most cultures the night sky has always abounded in human drama and symbolism: the striking summertime constellation of Orion, for example, represented an intrepid hunter in many diverse societies. And the Pleiades – which the Greeks mythologised as seven sisters changed first into doves and then stars – have also received startlingly parallel interpretations in various parts of the world. If anything can reconcile the human inhabitants of this planet, it may well be our eventual recognition that, under the canopy of the night sky we are all equal: how could egos that prance absurdly in the daylight fail to be awed and humbled by the magnificence of the stars – if it were not for the light pollution of our cities?[13]

The seed for this work was planted when Edwards accompanied a group of astronomers to outback Queensland on a star-gazing expedition, and it was Fred Watson, Astronomer-in-charge at the Anglo-Australian Telescope, who provided a kind of 'map', *The Astronomy of Star Chant*, which the symphony follows and which gives it its form.

Star Chant has a similar trajectory to *Da Pacem Domine* and both begin quietly with prominent use of the insistent rising and falling semitone. But where the earlier work is grounded in human ritual, *Star Chant* evokes the (to us) timeless repetitions of the 'majestic clock-work'; unlike *Da Pacem Domine*, *Star Chant* finds a place for passages of extravagant, glittering energy.

The work requires a chorus who sing the names − in the languages of various cultures − of the celestial features depicted in the music. Edwards explained to Rachel Kohn that:

> You've got the Indigenous peoples' view of the sky, of the southern sky specifically, and also the European and Arabic words for our local sky. And [Fred Watson] put them side by side, which I thought was a wonderful idea. So I made it into a chant in which these words are literally just repeated with appropriate music in the background. Had I done it any other way, it wouldn't have made sense to me. It really goes back to the piece I wrote in 1986 or 1987, called *Flower Songs*. Again I was stuck for a text. It was a commission from the Sydney Chamber Choir and I just grabbed a book of Australian wildflowers, and took some of the names that I liked out of it. And so it was a piece which for me was about flowers, but it wasn't descriptive, it was just chanting the names. And I did the same with the sky.[14]

Edwards is far from being arch here. His 'chanting the names' has a ritual element, and for him both ritual and music are about healing. Contemplation of the heavens is a cure for those 'egos that prance absurdly in the daylight' sowing conflict; this work, dedicated to Edwards' wife Helen, is also perhaps a reminder of Dante's sublime final image in the *Divine Comedy* of 'the love that moves the sun and other stars'.

Paul Stanhope: An Optimistic, Personal Geography

In 2004 Paul Stanhope's *Fantasia on a Theme by Vaughan Williams* was awarded first place in the 2004 Tōru Takemitsu Composition Prize and performed by the Tokyo Philharmonic on 30 May of that year. The prize was richly deserved, as Stanhope's piece is an example of excellent craftsmanship. Orchestration isn't rocket science and can be effectively taught and mastered, but it is remarkable how often contemporary composers fall into the traps of poor balance between orchestral sections and unidiomatic writing for specific instruments. Stanhope never does: the orchestration of this work is always lucid, we can always hear what's meant to be happening in the music, and the individual instrumental lines never sound strained or awkward.

The selection of this work for the Takemitsu prize also showed how much the culture of contemporary music had changed over the previous three decades. There is a certain quiet radicalism to this work: a gifted composer of the early 21st century ransacks an early twentieth century hymn-book at a time when conventional religion is being sidetracked by New Age spirituality and multiplex happy-clappy evangelicalism. He chooses as his theme an Anglican hymn tune (*Down Ampney*) by Ralph Vaughan Williams, who has often been written off as merely peddling a nostalgic English pastoralism. Further, while Anglicanism enjoys a certain historical eminence in Australia, gone are the days when one could assume that most listeners would recognise such a hymn tune (and by implication its words). Moreover, while composers (regardless of sectarian stripe) throughout western history have occasionally appropriated Gregorian chant, those who have used the hymn (or chorale) have tended to be squarely in the Protestant tradition: Bach's treatment of chorales was often deliberately 'affective' and theatrical but always reverent. Mendelssohn's and Brahms' more sober use of chorales sought to align their work with the tradition that Bach represents, while the US maverick Charles Ives used the popular hymn to depict the youthful energy of American culture. Vaughan Williams himself, of course, composed a masterpiece in his own *Fantasia on a theme by Thomas Tallis*, using one of the Tudor composer's psalm tunes. Stanhope's use of a hymn isn't unheard of among contemporary Australians: Brett Dean quotes the tune sung to 'O Brother Man' to ironic purpose in his *Dispersal*; Raffaele Marcellino's (born 1964) tuba concerto *On Eagle's Wings* plays lovingly with *Slane*, best known as 'Be thou my vision'.

Stanhope has composed in most traditional genres, and it's possible to see some recurring concerns in his work. He has, for instance, an ongoing interest in the music and culture of Aboriginal Australia – notably in the series of 'Morning Star' chamber works based on the *Mularra* clan-song series owned by the Rembarrnga-speaking people of North Central Arnhem Land; the oboe and harp concerto *Yanihndi* (2003); and his settings of poetry by Oodgeroo Noonuccal, *Songs for the Shadowland* (1999). Several pieces also base themselves on earlier works of western music: the recent piano trio *Dolcissimo uscignolo* (2007) refers to a Monteverdi madrigal, and the short piano quartet '*My song is love unknown*' prefigures the 'Vaughan Williams Fantasia' in its sectional structure and examination of a hymn tune, in this case one by John Ireland.

Stanhope was drawn to Ireland's tune 'because of its sense of compassion and pathos, rather than out of religious affiliation'.[15] Love is also the theme of the text of the hymn sung to *Down Ampney*, 'Come down, O Love Divine', written by Italian poet Bianco da Siena (died 1434). It was translated into English by an Anglo-Irish priest, Richard Frederick Littledale, and included, with Vaughan Williams' tune, in the *English Hymnal* of 1906. It is a hymn to the Holy Spirit, whose gift of celestial fire has often been identified with imaginative inspiration. (Ross Edwards' use of the *Veni creator spiritus* chant in his string octet of the same name is a recent Australian case in point.) In Bianco's poem inspiration is described metaphorically as 'clothing'; this perhaps offers an insight into the various vestures in which Stanhope dresses Vaughan Williams' theme.

The *Fantasia on a Theme by Vaughan Williams* is scored for a standard symphony orchestra with an enlarged percussion section. It falls into six contrasting sections, though is played without a break (and indeed, Stanhope is careful to blur the lines between sections). In the first, 'Fanfares', we hear what Stanhope calls an 'heraldic exposition of the theme'. It begins with a burst of energy, rippling and swirling figurations supporting more emphatic brass statements as well as tubular bells which pick out the characteristic opening motif of the tune. The sound world is reminiscent of Carl Vine's *MicroSymphony*; similarly Andrew Ford's *The Unquiet Grave* brightly etches important thematic material in bell tones at the opening. The opening phrase of the melody is a rising pentatonic figure (in C major: C D E G A). This sequence of notes has great importance to both melody and harmony throughout the work. Its rhythm (minim, crotchet, crotchet, minim, minim, semibreve) is also pervasive, even when unmoored from its original harmony.

Stanhope in no way attempts to mimic Vaughan Williams' own style, except perhaps in minor details like the occasional use of triplets (over one or two beats) towards the end of a phrase. The hymn's text asks for something which hasn't yet been granted, and perhaps for this reason the optimistic elements of Stanhope's piece are often undercut by gestures which suggest collapse. In this first section, for instance, he uses falling quarter-tone glissandos. Later in the piece these will extend over a greater range and assume more significance. The first section also establishes the degree of plasticity that Stanhope has found in the theme: at one point (letter A in the score) flutes in semiquavers play a version of the tune before the heraldic music returns. Here, interpolations from the brass are immediately recognisable as the contours and rhythms of the theme, but with a kind of 'wrong-note' harmony. Some light finally shines through in serene wind homophony but is interrupted by gruff chromaticism from low strings.

This leads into the second 'Lugubrious' section where, as Stanhope puts it, 'sighing string lines accompany an augmented and decorated version of the hymn tune in paired woodwinds'. This species counterpoint gives way to a rising passage where the first five notes of the theme cycle through a number of key areas. The upward soaring is, however, interrupted by what the composer calls 'foreboding figures in the brass and percussion'. As before, these last moments of the section prefigure the mood of the section to come, which is simply headed 'Percussive'. Tom-toms, bongos and timpani iterate strongly profiled semiquaver ostinatos, while woodwinds and trumpets respond with staccato bitonal chords in quavers which outline motifs derived from the hymn tune. Trombones play a short motif from the second half of the tune in long notes. The relentless beat of this musical paragraph is briefly undermined by a foray into $\frac{5}{8}$ metre, and then by what Stanhope calls a 'devilish marimba solo accompanied by pizzicato strings' in which the harmony is based on the interval of the perfect fourth. There is a fragmentary, serene memory of the hymn before the ostinatos return. In keeping with the dramatic pattern established earlier, the section climaxes with trombone glissandos that are taken up by the strings, as the music fades into the next section.

The fourth section is itself subdivided into 'Photo Negative' ('the complete opposite of the previous section') and 'Chorales with Walking Bass'. After the obsessive energy of 'Percussive', 'Photo Negative' offers a kind of suspended animation: the cor anglais has a serpentine figure while other woodwinds play very soft, usually simple semitonal motifs at the extremes of their range. Muted trumpets create a static harmony against strange delicate washes from one suspended cymbal played with a double bass bow and another placed upside-down on timpani as that instrument's skin-tension is modified by the player. There is an inevitably Stravinskian flavour to the strikingly voiced wind sonorities reminding us of the importance of wind instruments in 'spiritual' contexts, (especially for Stravinsky in the *Symphony of Psalms* or Mass) and indeed, out of this frozen state, recognisable fragments of the theme emerge. At the same time, though, a pizzicato bass-line in a new metre and hi-hat cymbals gradually lead into 'Chorales with Walking Bass'. The 'walking bass' is of course a feature of both baroque music and jazz, and here Stanhope cultivates both. At first the winds maintain a hieratic calm, with long breathed, glowing homophony while the percussion (including vibraphone) and bass assert a more profane aesthetic. The 'profane' music wins out with four splendidly louche bars of big band music at the end of the section.

It's a measure of Stanhope's touch that this genuinely funny gesture doesn't outstay its welcome. It is summarily brushed aside by 'Fanfares Reprise', with urgent short semiquaver figures in the strings, rapidly curling scale figures in the winds and full-throated phrases from the brass. In Stanhope's words 'the pent up energy explodes into a joyful climax' where motifs from the hymn tune are presented in counterpoint: the slow-moving chorale-like statement, for instance, is accompanied by the opening of the tune in string semiquavers, followed immediately by yet another rhythmic version from the horns. As we might expect, though, the restatement of the opening fanfare leads into a 'descent into chaos', a passage of aleatoric texture which gradually fades.

In a majority of works Vaughan Williams closes with a contemplative epilogue, and here Stanhope follows his lead. 'Hymn' gives us the first uninterrupted statement of the tune's opening phrases in simple modal harmony, gently punctuated by the sounds of distant bells. A pair of flutes in quavers is added; other woodwinds, celesta and metal percussion use the opening five-note motif to create quiet stairways to heaven. The motif itself conflates into a shining five-note chord reminiscent of the 'Lux aeterna' finale of Benjamin Britten's *Sinfonia da requiem*, and looks forward to the more recent, soft-edged *Cloudforms* (2007). But, as we've seen, the moods of this piece again and again prove transient, and in his final gesture Stanhope brings us brutally back to earth.

Stanhope has written that his 'music presents the listener with an optimistic, personal geography ... whether this is a reaction to the elemental aspects of the universe (both the celestial and terrestrial) or the throbbing energy of the inner-city.'[16] The *Fantasia on a Theme by Vaughan Williams* reflects this generous, encompassing aesthetic. It is in Stanhope's own words a 'rhetorical' piece, but it is a very self-aware rhetoric: those deflations, glissandos and descents into chaos make sure the rhetoric never becomes empty.

Chapter 9

Ex Patria

We have discussed musicians who immigrated to Australia in the nine-teenth and early twentieth centuries, and the influence of composers who arrived here as refugee children or young adults after World War II. More recently, an important figure, Bozidar Kos (born 1934), arrived here in the 1960s and went on to teach in Adelaide (in the 1970s) and then Sydney (from 1983 to 2002) while maintaining an international reputation. Elena Kats-Chernin arrived from the then Soviet Union as a teenager in 1975; Julian Yu (born 1957) left China for Australia a decade later. From the 1970s on, more composers from abroad who were already established in their profession chose to make Australia their home base. Sometimes this was more by accident than design. Roger Smalley (born 1943), for instance, initially came to Australia as a visiting composer in residence with the University of Western Australia in 1974 and returned, briefly, to the United Kingdom. It was only a year or so later though that he was back in Perth, and he has remained in Australia ever since. Tristram Cary (1925–2008) similarly came to Australia, settling in Adelaide, in the 1970s having established himself as a pioneer of electronic music, a prolific composer of music for film and television as well as serious works for the concert stage and a fine writer on music. Both Smalley and Cary were invaluable additions to the institutions for which they worked, but they also maintained their international reputations and thus enhanced Australia's musical standing.

Of a younger generation, Chris Dench (born 1953) emigrated from the UK in 1988 and has since enjoyed a certain notoriety as an exponent of the 'new complexity' (though just how that might differ from the old complexity remains a mystery). His work, much championed by the Elision ensemble, has been performed at contemporary music festivals around the world. Another British-born composer is Andrew Ford (born 1957), who came to Australia, like Smalley and Cary, to take up an academic position in 1983. Ford has since become one of Australia's most important commentators on music, through ABC radio programs such as *Illegal Harmonies* and *Dots on the Landscape*, and *The Music Show* on Radio National, as well as in a series of invaluable books on a huge range of musical subjects. His own work is as wide-ranging as his writing and broadcasting, embracing folk music, the Beatles and waltzes and covering several operas, orchestral pieces and much vocal music. It is perhaps a measure of Australian music's relaxed cosmopolitanism that Ford's viola concerto *The Unquiet Grave* reflects on an English folk tune without sounding like music of a nostalgic colonial. Those composers writing Asian-inflected music now include people, like Lim and Yu, of Asian heritage. Similarly, there are composers writing Australian music that reflects the migrant experience from a personal point of view, such as Constantine Koukias in his opera *To Traverse Water*. Georges Lentz, who divides his time between composition and playing violin in the Sydney Symphony Orchestra, is one of several composers from different generations who have matured in Australia having immigrated to this country; the same might be said of his SSO colleague Lee Bracegirdle (born 1952), a US-born horn player and composer in works like his *Ammerseelieder* (2005), of post-Schoenbergian lushness.

It was, as we've seen, common for promising Australian musicians to go abroad for further study, and a significant number stayed away. Of these, though, a subset retained a passionate sense of their Australian-ness: Grainger springs immediately to mind, despite the fact that he never, strictly speaking, held Australian citizenship. Born a 'British subject' before Australia's Federation in 1901, he ultimately became a citizen of the United States where he is, not unreasonably, claimed as an American composer. Malcolm Williamson departed these shores in 1950 for further study with serialist composers Elisabeth Lutyens and Erwin Stein, and acceptance into the hierarchy of British music led to his appointment as the first non-British Master of The Queen's Music in 1975. He nonetheless protested that most of his music was Australian, though specifically depicting the 'brashness of the cities'. Like Williamson, David Lumsdaine travelled to Britain in the 1950s and stayed on to take up a series of academic positions; unlike Williamson, though, Lumsdaine's music celebrates landscape rather than cityscape. This is evident in 'site-specific' works like *Shoalhaven* and *Salvation Creek with Eagle* and, as we have noted earlier, in the pervasive use of Australian birdsong in his music.

In the following sections we'll look at two composers – Smalley and Ford – who came to Australia from Britain. We and they were much changed as a result.

Roger Smalley and the Fear that Eats the Soul

In 1974 Roger Smalley accepted the invitation of Professor Frank Callaway to become composer in residence at the University of Western Australia for three months. It was a coup for the university and the city, as Smalley had established a significant reputation by then as composer, pianist and critic. After his residency Smalley returned to the UK but after two years was back in Perth, first as a research fellow and then as Associate Professor of Music at UWA.

Smalley has referred to one work composed between his two periods of residence in Perth as his 'real opus 1': *Accord* for two pianos. Smalley's post-*Accord* music contemplates the implications of non-diatonic chords and draws these out into a musical fabric. Each chord has a strong character and degree of dissonance; using the intervals of the chord to create horizontal lines – melody and counterpoint – underlines that relative degree of dissonance or consonance at any given point in the music. In a number of works, Smalley has explored the 'horizontal' implications of harmonic material from music by Chopin and Brahms, showing how fertile his imagination is in this area. A work like *Poles Apart*, for instance, takes some harmonic material from a work of Chopin and 'abstracts' it, never actually quoting the original.

The later 1970s, the time of Smalley's settling in Western Australia, were, as he put it to Mark Coughlan, 'rather thin compositionally'.[1] Perth has always been the most isolated city in the world, and 'whereas in London there were separate and knowledgeable audiences for new music, for early music, for choral music and so on, in Perth there was only one audience and these people attended everything'. Writing for this more broadly based, but enthusiastic, audience – Perth Festival concerts featuring composers as different as Harrison Birtwistle and Arvo Pärt have been howling successes – had its effect on Smalley's outlook in perhaps much the same way as a British artist like Blanchflower would have been blown away by the clarity and strength of the light in Western Australia.

Smalley assimilated the new directions which became apparent in *Accord* and which brought forth a new profusion of work in the following decades. He revisited some of *Accord*'s material in the Symphony in 1981; his first Piano Concerto (commissioned by the BBC for the European Music Year in 1985) was submitted by the ABC to the annual UNESCO Rostrum of Composers in 1987 where it earned the distinction of being named the 'recommended work'.

Diptych: Homage to Brian Blanchflower

September 1991 saw the first performances of *Diptych: Homage to Brian Blanchflower* which Smalley had begun the previous year. The premiere was given by the West Australian Symphony Orchestra under Jorge Mester – fittingly, not just because of Smalley's being a resident of Perth, but because Smalley had formed and become artistic director of the WASO's New Music Ensemble in 1989. We should note that until then there was no ensemble of that size (the same as the 14-piece London Sinfonietta line-up) working regularly in this country. Smalley's initiative meant the introduction of new works from overseas and the commissioning of new works for the ensemble from Australian composers.

So the *Diptych* was written for an orchestra with which Smalley was intimately familiar, and it was inspired by the work of a friend. Brian Blanchflower had also immigrated to Perth from the UK in the 1970s and, as Smalley has said, the work of both artist and composer was 'deeply affected' by the translation. In the two movements of his diptych, Smalley responds musically to works from two distinct periods of Blanchflower's output. As Smalley put it in 1991:

> I was particularly struck by the contrast between the extremely sombre series of paintings generically entitled *Nocturne* and the sculptural installation *Tursiops* (both dating from the early 80s) and the brilliant explosions of colour in his more recent work, typified by the painting *Glimpses (An Earth History)* of 1986–7. I envisaged a pair of orchestral pieces which would similarly embody this contrast between dark and light – contrasts which could be further extended in the musical domain to encompass polarities such as low/high, soft/loud, slow/fast, and statis/motion. It seemed obvious to give such a work the painterly title of *Diptych*.[2]

The work is written for large orchestra with a percussion section expanded to include sand drum (or geophone, an invention of Olivier Messiaen's which we also find in Liza Lim's *The Compass*) which blends with the sounds of a pre-recorded tape. The first 'panel' or movement,

Tursiops, 1981–83, the installation by Brian Blanchflower which inspired the first movement of Roger Smalley's *Diptych*. Photo by Brian Blanchflower used by permission, State Art Collection, State Gallery of Western Australia. Oil and bitumen on canvas, metal, wood, hessian, reeds and rope, with dolphin skull, sand, wax and chalk.

'Sea-nocturne', responds to the *Nocturne* paintings and the *Tursiops* installation. *Tursiops* is Latin for dolphin, and Blanchflower explains in his curatorial notes that he found and buried a dead dolphin on Cheyne Beach on the south coast of Western Australia and two years later exhumed its skeleton as a kind of talisman; he also notes that the southern coast of Western Australia had a long history of commercial whaling. The installation, which Blanchflower describes as a symbolic journey, consists of seven black objects incised with white marks (in multiples of seven) and arranged from left to right.

The first 'panel' of Smalley's *Diptych* consists of seven analogous sections.

1) *a square canvas on the wall*

Forearm clusters from the piano feel like a body blow; the orchestra's bass instruments snarl a low E as the timpani sound seven baleful crotchets that outline a major seventh (E flat) and the diminished fifth, or tritone (B flat). The piano quietly creates rapid figurations in its lower register, an effect like ink in water. Trilling strings create a sense of expectant tension, boosted by insistent low brass interjections and building to a climactic $\frac{7}{4}$ bar. Smalley's response to the work 'depicts the dark night in which "fear eats the soul" and is pervaded by the mysterious and threatening sounds of the nocturnal sea'.

2) *fourteen small baskets filled with sand plus a dolphin's skull arranged in a line on the floor*

Vertiginous downward runs from woodwinds, bedded in cluster chords from the strings represent the 'teeming profusion of detail [which] mirrors the complex granular surface of the two canvases in the installation'. Terse punctuating chords form an analogue of 'the white marks ... which stand out in relief against these textural backgrounds'. This soon gives way to slow, fluttering brass chords and a 'popping' texture of pizzicato strings created by limited aleatoricism: each string player must play a certain number of notes per beat, but these can be selected at his or her discretion from anywhere within a certain band of pitches. Fast-moving, randomly repeated figures in the bass clarinets and a susurrus of cymbal and geophone appear, before the orchestra subsides, through two $\frac{7}{4}$ bars, again into the depths.

3) a thin pole leaning against the wall

The short third section begins with the forearm cluster from the piano, which then articulates its version of the 'white' chords as a quiet, misty texture rises through winds and gliding, muted strings.

Roger Smalley: *Diptych*, bars 48–49. The piano chords represent the white marks which stand out dramatically in Brian Blanchflower's *Tursiops* installation. Used by permission of the composer.

4) an inverted triangular canvas on the wall

The following section, representing a triangular canvas, emerges from a cavernous interval. Like surreal birds or short-wave signals, violins play high artificial harmonics and rapid glissandos as the higher woodwinds rise and fall chromatically through the interval of the fourth. As the music becomes more and more feverish, the timpani sounds a version of its initial, ominous seven-note pattern leading to the section's climax – a searingly loud Bartókian chord; the music completes the triangle with a new perspective on the material with which the section began.

5) a military stretcher, without its canvas, leaning against the wall

The fifth section starts with high-lying string chords, later joined by woodwinds which play rapid crescendos as the piano and brass revisit their short, acerbic 'white' chords. This issues in a march section, marked 'relentless', scored for brass and tom-toms at first but accruing ever more insistent, repeated rhythmic figures from winds, drums and high strings. These emphatic rhythmic tattoos in winds and brass dominate the short, sixth section ...

6) *a string running down the wall from a small cross and sprouting seven cross-strings on the floor*

... as the strings slide slowly into darkening depths where trombones sound an ominous G minor-ish call.

7) *a looming shape reminiscent of a ship's keel, also on the floor*

The final section begins with a drone on E flat and a passage of haunting beauty, the payoff after the soul-eating fear that's gone before. Clarinets and horns create a heterophonic texture: all in the same narrow register, the simple pentatonic lines echo and gently clash, creating a sense of waves in endless space. Moving through different tonal centres and adding more sections of the orchestra, this builds up a texture of great richness, over the top of which Smalley crafts a silvery, expansive melody for the first violins and flute. Inevitably this combination in the context of sea music evokes the 'Dawn' interlude from Britten's *Peter Grimes*, an effect amplified towards the movement's end by the doubling of pizzicato strings and glockenspiel, which recalls the splashes of colour in Britten's 'Moonlight' interlude. The section fades into the ominous timbre of soft tam-tams, geophone and the sounds of air blown through the brass instruments over a dying pedal E flat, an analogue perhaps of TS Eliot's menacing image of 'the dark cold and the empty desolation, the wave cry, the wind cry, the vast waters of the petrel and porpoise'.[3]

In complete contrast to the stark monochrome of the *Tursiops* installation, the second panel of Smalley's *Diptych* is about colour and energy.

'Particle Madness' takes its title from a small canvas of Blanchflower's, but the music is inspired more by his larger *Glimpses (An Earth History)*. Blanchflower himself has written that the painting:

> epitomises the long process of building up complex masses of paint/energy, mark by mark, 'particle' by 'particle'. Here matter is in a constant state of flux, but one can glimpse embedded in it archetypal figures and the traces of past events. Forms disintegrate and in doing so reveal many layers of 'history', the various stages which the paint-ing went through over a period of two years.[4]

Smalley's 'Particle Madness' begins with another Britten-ish touch: a glinting dyad of C and E (suggesting an un-besmirched C major) on harp and vibraphone, the sound sustained by soft harmonics on cellos. (Britten uses this sound in Act II of *A Midsummer Night's Dream* where its connotations of magic are clear.) Like some fantastic magpie call, muted trumpets add short bursts of chromatic heterophony; flute, piccolo and harp embark on a long melody of wide intervals. The harmony gradually adds thirds above and below the C/E dyad, spread-ing through the string section, enlivened by trills. The melodic material begins to move ever faster. In fact, the momentum of the movement is towards faster and more elaborate textures. Contrapuntal lines for two bassoons, oboe and trumpet gather strength as a triplet figure moves into and dominates the strings, forming a new faster section in $\frac{3}{4}$. This metre is articulated by pizzicato violins doubling marimba. Against this faster crotchet pulse, flutes and other string lines add muscular figures in quavers. The $\frac{3}{4}$ pattern imperceptibly turns into triplets again as the speed ratchets down to the previous tempo. Flutes and oboes have unison melodies full of major thirds and tritones, as the strings maintain the driven triplet figures and trumpets weigh in with crisp, dry, muted fanfares. These figures, transferred to the wood-winds and timpani, accompany longer lines from the trombones over an even slower moving bass line. There is finally a section where the whole orchestra becomes a web of strongly profiled rhythmic figures; the 'particle madness' of the title is perfectly realised precisely because the composer's ear makes sure that no detail obscures another. This acuity is evident in the masterly deployment of orchestral mass and colour, just as it is in Smalley's beautifully imagined chamber and solo works.

Andrew Ford and *The Unquiet Grave*

You'll know Andrew Ford if you're a fan of *The Music Show* on ABC Radio National, where he discusses an amazing range of music and talks to an amazing range of musicians. The title of his most recent collection of interviews, *Talking to Kinky and Karlheinz*, says it all; Ford is genuinely enthusiastic and knowledgeable about all the music he discusses, be it that of Texas' only Jewish cowboy or the late Meister of the German avant-garde. He has also broadcast important radio series, among them *Dots on the Landscape* (available as streamed audio from ABC Classic FM's website) which is an invaluable oral history of Australian music. He has published a book of interviews, *Composer to Composer*, a study of Van Morrison (co-authored by Martin Buzacott), and the heartfelt *In Defence of Classical Music*. But as he would point out, the writing and broadcasting is part of his principal vocation, which is as a composer – and a prolific one at that.

Like Roger Smalley, Ford was born and educated in Britain and came to Australia to take up an academic position – in his case, at the University of Wollongong in 1983. And, as in Smalley's case, it is fair to say that being in Australia caused the composer's work to take a direction he might not have foreseen. It is not that Ford or Smalley became any more 'conservative' than they might have been had they stayed in the UK. But conditions such as the number and nature of opportunities and the size and expectations of audiences here are different. It's not just that there are fewer concerts or more conservative audiences: in fact, as Roger Smalley found in Perth, the difference is partly that Australian audiences were more generalist, going to everything on offer be it baroque or Birtwistle. The emphasis is different, and, inevitably, so is the music.

UNSW PRESS

with compliments

POSTAL ADDRESS

UNSW PRESS
University of New South Wales
Sydney NSW 2052 Australia

COURIERS + VISITORS

Cliffbrook Campus
45 Beach Street
Coogee NSW 2034

DISTRIBUTION CENTRE

Corner Govett St & Govett Lane
Randwick NSW 2031

FACSIMILE	(02) 9664 5420 (office)
	(02) 9385 0155 (distribution centre)
INTERNATIONAL	+61 2 9664 5420

GENERAL	(02) 9664 0900
CUSTOMER SERVICE	(02) 9385 0150
ACCOUNTS	(02) 9664 0901
MARKETING	(02) 9664 0902
EDITORIAL	(02) 9664 0935
PRODUCTION	(02) 9664 0937

The sources of Ford's work are as varied as the guests he profiles each Saturday morning. His vocal music sets texts by, for instance, Christina Rossetti, Thomas Campion, Goethe, St John of the Cross, AD Hope and Sappho (that's for just the text for one work) or Malay, Finnish and Pueblo Indian folk poetry (that's for one other). His interest in language has made him a prolific composer of music-theatre works, ranging from pieces written for young performers through to adult concepts like the monodramas *Night and Dreams*, about Sigmund Freud, *Casanova Confined* or *Whispers*, in which a conductor experiences mental collapse while rehearsing Mahler's Fourth Symphony. There are larger-scale operas too, such as *Poe* and *Rembrandt's Wife*. The visual arts are another major source of inspiration. In his *Manhattan Epiphanies*, a set of stand-alone works composed for the 17 solo strings of the Australian Chamber Orchestra, Ford responds with musical analogues to the creative techniques in artworks by Rothko, Cornell and Motherwell; a number of other pieces celebrate the works of Mondrian and Brueghel.

Ford's greatest inspiration comes, however, from music itself and this is reflected in a generous eclecticism. His Piano Concerto: *Imaginings* alludes to the Mersey sound of the popular music in Ford's native Liverpool; *Whispers*, as we have noted, fades in and out of Mahler. But a further influence runs like a thread through much of Ford's music: that of folk song. As he has noted, in 1985:

> When I was commissioned by a British music-theatre company to write an evening-long work that would draw on the earliest recollections – including musical recollections – of elderly people living in the Yorkshire Dales, I was surprised to discover memories of the folk songs I'd known as a child coming back to me very strongly. Added to this was a new awareness, on my part, of a tradition of fiddling still relatively healthy in parts of the Dales. At least it was in 1985.[5]

The music-theatre work was *Hand to Mouth*, a relatively site-specific piece, but three tunes from it found their way into *On Canaan's Happier Shore* composed for Elision in 1987. In this work, as in subsequent ones, the folk material isn't merely quoted and 'set': it forms the basis for abstracted development. Ford took this a step further in *Pastoral* for string octet, where the instrumental figurations owe much to, but do not merely replicate, traditional fiddling styles. In *Dance Maze*, similarly, the metres and rhythms of dance create a sense of something half remembered, of dancers lifting heavy feet in clumsy shoes. The echoes of folk styles reverberate in works like *Tales of the Supernatural*, in both the string writing and the construction of melodies. In his concerto for viola and chamber orchestra, *The Unquiet Grave*, Ford gradually reassembles a classic English folk song.

Until quite recently anything that resembled the work of 'English pastoral' composers – say, Vaughan Williams or Butterworth – was regarded as irredeemably retro nostalgia. Australian composers such as Robert Hughes (1912–2007) or Clive Douglas (1903–1977) whose music retained traces of a British accent were, from the 1970s on, seen as a symptom of the cultural cringe to be laughed off the stage by real modernists. Thankfully, the conversation about 'Australian' music has finished with narrow notions of nationality and it is a sign of some maturity that this material is now available without the cultural baggage. In this context, it is worth noting that Ford's *Dance Maze* received its premiere performance abroad: Australian music can easily embrace a British-born composer using English folk material for a work to be premiered in the United States.

'The Unquiet Grave' is a folk tune that was collected in 1868, well before the English folk-song revival spearheaded by Ralph Vaughan Williams, Gustav Holst and, indeed, Percy Grainger. (It is also the title of a book of wartime meditations by Cyril Connolly about 'the core of melancholy and guilt that works destruction on us from within', which Ford had read at about the time he began composing the work.) The ballad tells the story of a young man whose lover has been slain in the forest and whom he (though the roles can of course be reversed) mourns 'for a twelve-month and a day'. After this time the ghost of his dead love arises, pointing out that his grief is preventing her from resting in peace. She tells him that to kiss him now would kill him, but that they will meet again 'when the autumn leaves that fall from the trees/ are green and spring up again'.

Like Benjamin Britten in a number of works based on existing melodies, Ford contrives to save a full statement of the tune until the end, a reversal of the classical pattern of 'theme and variations'. The experience of the piece is a process of discovering something, piecing together fragments of the tune, or seeing its contour flattened or expanded according to the prevailing mood. *The Unquiet Grave* does not seek to replicate the events of the poem in any programmatic way, but its orchestration evokes the shivering cold, and the extreme emotional states of the ballad's singer. These range from the bleak melancholy of the opening, through nostalgic reminiscence and smudged outbursts of frank anger. We might 'hear' the voice of the ghost in some of the viola writing, and even see the eventual statement of the tune as the attainment of calm acceptance, if not comfort.

Ford's concerto is scored for solo viola and a mixed ensemble of 14 instruments including saxophone (soprano and alto), which blends admirably with the viola. A three-note (E flat-G-F) motif, drawn from the folk tune, opens the piece. Winds and trumpet mask the beginning of the horn's long E flat with a dry staccato – not hearing the attack of a note affects how we perceive its tone quality; it can make it initially difficult to recognise the instrument playing, giving the sound a literally disembodied quality. Over the horn, tubular bells and harp provide the remaining G–F, the latter note left hanging like a faint echo as a double bass harmonic. Other strings add harmonics to create a cold, misty chord, as the soloist begins with a motif that gradually widens out from knotted semitones and tones to fifths, sixths and a falling minor ninth, like watching a flower unfold in time-lapse photography. In this way Ford establishes the icy sound-world and emotional temperature of the piece.

The viola's journey through this landscape encompasses extremes – long and soulful melodies, an almost silent wailing of harmonics far above the texture. A new section has leaping disjunct patterns, echoed by the alto saxophone, while the orchestral viola sings a wide-ranging

Andrew Ford: *The Unquiet Grave*, bars 3–5. A characteristic melodic pattern begins with tight intervals that gradually expand outwards.
Used by permission of the composer.

melody; the solo part becomes more angular with hacking double- and triple-stopped fragments that break eventually into liquid sextuplet lines.

At one climactic moment the viola's high expansive melody is doubled at pitch by repeated sextuplets on vibraphone, adding a throbbing vibrancy to the sound. Soon swirling string figures and harp glissandos sound before the downbeat of each new bar; the viola finally reaches the F above the treble stave – the viola's sound here is necessarily tense, requiring a lot of pressure and control from the player's left hand. The tension shatters the music into fragments: pizzicato quavers, staccato writing for flute, oboe and harp, short dry cluster chords from trumpet, horn and vibraphone. The viola returns to earth with heavy bowing in its lowest register, effortfully rising again against static wind writing and taking the viola back to its highest extremes. In the following cadenza the viola shudders with ghostly *sul ponticello* (near the bridge) bowing. A single note from the horn tries to bring the music back to reality – we expect the bell to answer as at the start, but only a brusque staccato chord, sounded three times by the harp, releases the glacial string chords and a melody on piccolo derived from the viola's very first motif.

The horn, bell and harp gesture returns at double speed; a frenzied passage dominated by fretful repeated notes in the horn and trumpet and surging, microtonal thrusts from the strings presents a musical image of hysterical grief. In the hollow space left by the inevitable collapse, supported only by a double bass harmonic and soft, slow-moving lines from the brass and wind, the viola quietly sings phrases from the original tune (the score includes the words: 'Cold blows the wind to my true love, and gently drops the rain. I never had but one true love, and in the greenwood she lies slain'). The effect is a little like that described by Emily Dickinson in poem 341: 'After great pain, a formal feeling comes/ the nerves sit ceremonious like tombs.' The work ends as the melody unfolds, against gently falling scalar figures in the winds, and a soft string chord which implies, perhaps, G minor.

The Unquiet Grave is dedicated to the memory of British composer Michael Tippett who died around the time of the work's composition. Ford has approvingly quoted Tippett's desire to create 'images of reconciliation for worlds torn by division. And in an age of mediocrity and shattered dreams, images of abounding, generous, exuberant beauty.'[6] He has done just that in this work.

Chapter 10

Virtuoso Engendered

Music, it goes without saying, needs performers in order to flourish, and new music needs performers with a certain kind of dedication. John Hopkins, mentioned earlier in his role as director of music at the ABC from the early 1960s, was also an energetic promoter of new music as a conductor. Other Australian conductors who have made a particular point of supporting new music include Patrick Thomas, the late Stuart Challender, Roland Peelman and Simone Young, and we have been fortunate to have had resident international conductors such as David Porcelijn who have embraced this country's new music. Complementing the rise of dedicated contemporary music ensembles, a group of often charismatic soloists who welcomed the opportunity to perform new work began to emerge in the 1970s. It is impossible to do them all justice, but here we'll mention some of the most influential. Pianist Roger Woodward was among the first, establishing himself in Europe and giving first performances of works by major figures there. Australian composers whose work he has championed as a performer include Richard Meale, Anne Boyd, Peter Sculthorpe, Barry Conyngham, Alison Bauld (born 1944) and Larry Sitsky – a recent major work which Woodward premiered was Sitsky's long-awaited Concerto for Piano and Orchestra, *The Twenty-Two Paths of the Tarot*; he has also advocated new music as founder of Music Rostrum and the Sydney Spring International Festival of New Music. Woodward has been followed by a number of pianists equally friendly to new music. Michael Kieran Harvey has been the chosen vessel for several new works by Carl Vine (his piano sonatas and concerto) and numerous others. Ian Munro is a fine composer himself – his piano concerto *Dreams* won the 2003 Queen Elisabeth International Competition in Belgium and he has moreover premiered important new works by figures of the stature of Peter Sculthorpe and Andrew Ford. New York-based Lisa Moore has a particular association with a number of composers produced by the Sydney Conservatorium, premiering solo works by Elena Kats-Chernin, Gerard Brophy and Michael Smetanin; she recently premiered Smetanin's piano concerto *Mysterium cosmographicum* (2005). Stephanie McCallum has given the first performances of concertos by Kats-Chernin and many solo works. There are of course more such soloists. Each of those mentioned here has a distinctive style which has been embodied in the works composed for them: the almost hyperactive energy of Harvey and Moore, the cool precision of McCallum, the poetic sensitivity of Munro.

Among other instrumentalists we should mention the harpist Marshall McGuire, who has commissioned some twenty new works for his instrument; cellists Nathan Waks and David Pereira; the oboist Diana Doherty for whom Ross Edwards and Graeme Koehne have written major concertos. Edwards has since written a clarinet concerto for Melbourne's David Thomas but it is the viola which has had an unusual prominence in recent Australian music, having fine concertos written for it by Brett Dean, Georges Lentz and Andrew Ford. But there has also been a growing interest in concertos for less traditional instruments. We've noted the inspiring effect of William Barton's artistry on composers writing for didjeridu, that of Satsuki Odamura on koto, Riley Lee on shakuhachi and the rise of taiko drumming. Elena Kats-Chernin and James Ledger have both composed elegant concertos for recorder virtuoso Genevieve Lacey. Guitarists Slava and Leonard Grigoryan have performed new works, notably by Shaun Rigney and Nigel Westlake, and recently we have seen the emergence of Joseph Tawadros, a master of the *oud*, the Arabic precursor to the lute, who has worked with a number of 'western' performers.

Choirs throughout the country are taking up the challenge of new music: I have mentioned Astra, but the descendants of the old choral societies, especially Sydney Philharmonia and Melbourne Chorale, have done good work. The vocal sextet The Song Company, under Roland Peelman, has set musical agendas now for many years. Sydney-based Lyn Williams has created a formidable national children's choir in Gondwana Voices; composer Stephen Leek's Australian Voices is a youth-choir with an enviable reputation for performing new music. There are many Australian solo singers who frequently perform new work – a tradition that goes back to Melba – and Australia was favoured when Gerald English, a pioneer of both early and contemporary music, made his home in Melbourne in the late 1970s. Like him, many younger Australian singers are enthusiastic performers in new work for the stage, and some

Conductor Simone Young.
Photo by Bridget Elliot.

artists have become highly specialised: soprano Deborah Kayzer, for instance, is almost exclusively involved in the 'difficult' experimental work composed by the likes of David Young and Liza Lim. One of the most versatile singers is Merlyn Quaife, equally at home in standard repertoire as in the most demanding contemporary roles; mezzo-soprano Elizabeth Campbell is more likely than not to be found in any new operatic production.

In recent years we have also seen a rapid growth in instrument building in this country, with makers producing some of the finest

instruments of their type in the world. Genevieve Lacey's Ganassi recorder, discussed in the next section, was built by the late Fred Morgan. Morgan, who is the subject of a recent commemorative book[1], was a pioneer in researching old instruments and in 1975 built the Ganassi on the model of a late medieval instrument. Frans Brüggen was the first to take up the instrument, admiring it for its rich tone and extended range. There are dozens of excellent instrument makers[2], many using Australian timbers and making structural improvements in their designs. This extends to piano manufacture, with two notable workshops in this country. Ron Overs specialises in rebuilding pianos

Riley Lee, grand master of the shakuhachi. Photo by Bridget Elliot.

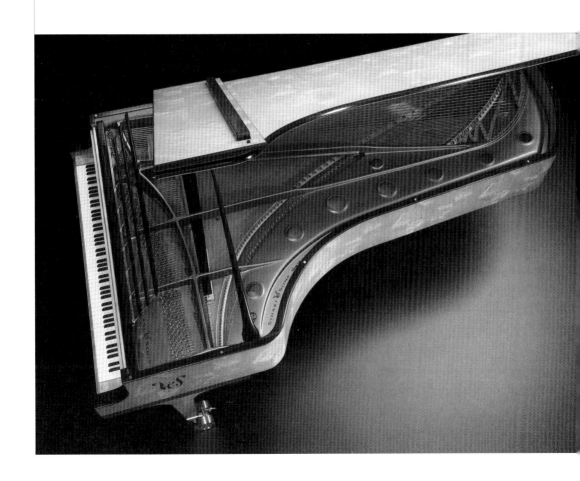

Handcrafted Australian piano by Stuart and Sons. Photo by Greg Devine.

with a newly designed keyboard action which he describes as having much less friction than usual, thus providing a smoother, more responsive touch. Wayne Stuart, by contrast, has begun building pianos with a whole new technology and produced a new sound. It tends to be bright and clear, even in the middle and bass registers; the instruments have a larger compass than standard, and Stuart pianos also have a fourth – effectively an extra 'soft' – pedal which further extends their range of colour.

There is an overwhelming number of fine makers of string instruments in this country. Luthiers like Greg Smallman have made significant innovations to building techniques resulting in instruments of increased tonal range and power, attracting the attention of performers like John Williams and the Canberra-based Guitar Trek, which uses a quartet of variously sized instruments. As Michael Hannan has noted, such endorsements have been of enormous importance to the makers and their craft.[3] Luthier Graham Caldersmith has also made orchestral instruments such as the cello for David Pereira for which Nigel Butterley wrote an inaugural piece. And as we'll see later in this book, Australian Bell has produced instruments which bring together thousands of years of craftsmanship and the latest computer-based technology.

Ledger Lines

The recorder seems to have been invented some time in the fourteenth century – at least, that is when the earliest surviving specimens were made. Its main advantage over the transverse flute – its nearest relative – is in the technology of the mouthpiece, where a wooden block focuses the player's airstream onto a sharp edge. This splits the airstream, whose oscillations produce the sound. A flautist does this by means of the embouchure, or position of the lips; the student recorder player can skip the step of learning to pucker up and can make a musical sound much sooner. Or that's the theory, undermined perhaps by the reality of the sound of primary school recorder bands. But of course, long before the mass-produced plastic recorder found its way into school rooms, the instrument had acquired a long and distinguished history and repertoire. It fell into desuetude in the late eighteenth century for a number of reasons. Its dynamic range, in an era of ever-larger ensembles and performance halls, is limited − simply blowing harder, as every schoolteacher knows, causes the instrument to go out of tune or to produce unwanted harmonics. And where the flute eventually gained a mechanical system of keys to allow the smooth, even production of chromatic notes, the recorder maintained the use of cross-fingering to produce notes outside the diatonic scale to which the instrument is tuned. Chromatic notes on the recorder are thus slightly more awkward to play and run the risk of being slightly out of tune.

Which makes it strange, perhaps, that one of Nigel Butterley's earliest and most enduring works, *The White-Throated Warbler*, is a serial (and therefore totally chromatic) work for recorder and harpsichord. Butterley wrote the piece in 1965 for Carl Dolmetsch, a recorder virtuoso and member of a family who led the twentieth century's early music revival; in the orchestral *Meditations of Thomas Traherne*, Butterley uses an ensemble of recorders to evoke the world of the 'little stranger', the poet as child. Since then the recorder has had a number of champions among Australian composers, being notably helped by the contributions of composer/performer Ian Shanahan whose works make use of extended techniques like multiphonics and cultivate the vagaries of non-tempered tuning made possible by cross-fingering. For dramatic effect, Damien Ricketson has his bass flautist play recorder in *Ptolemy's Onion*. In recent years the virtuoso Genevieve Lacey has had a number of concertos written for her, notably Elena Kats-Chernin's Bachian palimpsest, *Re-inventions* and James Ledger's *Line Drawing*.

Based in Perth, Ledger has established himself as a fine craftsman − he has extensive experience as an arranger − and a prolific and inventive composer. His orchestral music has been widely played throughout Australia and Europe, and he has recently been composer-in-residence with the West Australian Symphony Orchestra. Among his orchestral works are three concertos: for horn, for trumpet and *Line Drawing* for recorder. The two brass concertos are full-scale, three-movement works;

the Trumpet Concerto is also typical of Ledger in its use of evocative titles for its movements and wonderful ear for sound. *Line Drawing* is inevitably more modest in scale, though no less virtuosic or idiomatically written. Like Kats-Chernin's work, it is for recorder and strings so the recorder never has to hack its way through a dense orchestral sound. Ledger uses quite a lot of *flautato* (where the string player exerts very light pressure to produce a pale sound) writing as well as techniques like the white noise of *sul ponticello* and muting. Ledger also extends this palette by requiring the soloist to play bass, tenor, treble, descant, sopranino and 'G' Ganassi recorders. Not all at once, of course – although ...

Line Drawing is in a single movement but falls into six linked sections. The slow opening announces important thematic material with viola, cello and double bass lines in unison. The melodic rising motif of C, F, E flat, B, B flat has a distinct flavour: it suggests the tonality of C minor and implied dissonances (B – F, and B – C) that pervade the whole work. The tenor recorder's initial long note and wide vibrato, capped by a staccato note a step up, is itself an announcement of extended technique (the 'block' mechanism generally encourages a 'purer' sound) and contrasts with the deliberately cold sound of strings without vibrato. Throughout this section the solo part alternates long, but inflected, notes with free cadenza-like passages derived from the opening thematic material. Ledger is careful to use a blend of solo and tutti strings for maximum transparency; his characteristic harmony is established here as one built up from fourths with the spice of a minor sixth (G, F, C, A flat). The second section is faster, with a pattern of semiquavers in the first violin covering open fifths that rise by quarter-tone steps. This unstable shimmer is contrasted with a pithy, angular motif from viola and more long notes from the treble recorder. The cello has a melody derived from the opening theme that weaves through a texture dominated increasingly by broken chords in see-saw sextuplets, indeterminate glissandos in double bass and chirping rapid figures in the first violin and descant, then sopranino, recorder.

Genevieve Lacey, playing a Ganassi recorder built by the late Australian instrument maker, Fred Morgan. Photo by Elizabeth O'Donnell.

The third section is faster yet, and very sparely scored at first. The soloist alternates descant and sopranino instruments in lines which contrast long notes with short overblown multiphonics, punctuated by randomly pitched interjections from the strings. Ledger gradually adds more definitively pitched material, with string triplets in unison based on pitches from the first theme (here changed to C, B, C, E flat, F, E flat) which respond to the recorder's repeated C, E flat, B figure. The music gains tension as the triplets turn into more insistent figures of paired semiquavers on the beat.

The first four notes of the theme are given in emphatic unison by the strings, signalling the beginning of the fourth section, the most unstable and formally complex. The music feels as if it wants to return to the material of the previous section, but is dragged downward by a falling scale where it dissolves into a passage of controlled aleatoricism: the febrile texture is produced by basses, cellos and second violins playing arpeggios of open strings in free rhythm, supporting a high fluttering line for the soloist. This reaches a climax where the recorder's high staccato triplets, full of knotted semitone/tone figures, begin to include thirds. The triplets become quintuplets over a quivering string cluster and lead to a downward-tending cadenza before the prevailing tempo is reinstated. The recorder's semiquavers are phrased in pairs, and answered by staccato semiquavers in upper strings and the gradual infiltration of triplets in lower parts. Against evermore aggressive string rhythms the recorder (now descant) plays nervous quintuplets reiterating the B, F, C pattern implicit in the main theme. Again there is a passage of dissolving aleatoricism, pulling the soloist's line towards an implacable 'drumbeat' in the lower strings.

A lugubrious bass recorder solo against very slow-moving chords begins the fifth section. This is challenged by sudden, very much faster staccato figures in solo viola, but the instrument is both muted and playing *sul tasto*, guaranteed not to project too much. There is much semitone/tone twisting in rapid figurations in the bass recorder, echoed in the much slower-moving bass strings and contrasting with the plaintive outlining of the C minor triad in the first violins. There is a brief moment of flourishes for descant recorder against the prevailing tempo, before Ledger's *coup de théâtre*. Here the soloist plays descant *and* Ganassi recorder at the same time.

The Ganassi, as mentioned earlier, is a version of the instrument, characterised by large fingerholes, a wide bore and a flared bell, that has a warmer timbre and larger potential range than most recorders. Lacey's instrument was developed and made by Fred Morgan, and uses Aron (or Aaron) mean-tone tuning. (Unlike equal temperament, which is most commonly used today, mean-tone tuning doesn't make all the semitone intervals equal, so some intervals, like major thirds in common keys, are wider and therefore brighter in sound; the corollary is that some intervals, like E flat to G sharp, are no longer 'perfect' and sound weirdly out of tune – that one is nicknamed the 'wolf' because it howls.)

So when the Ganassi is used here in conjunction with an equal-tempered descant, there is genuine pathos – much as in Ligeti's Violin Concerto when a chorus of ocarinas suddenly emerges from the orchestral mass. The moment is fleeting though, as the soloist returns to the bass recorder for a cadenza in which the opening motif is pulled apart and reassembled with what the score directs should be a 'very "raw" sound' and which culminates in quick alternation of quarter-tones. A quick change to tenor recorder and we are in the work's short final section, marked 'with much despair'. A slow melody, where the tight semitone/tone patterns have been loosened slightly to include thirds and fourths, keens about a glacially moving harmony, based on chords formed from the superimposition of the opening motive (i.e. a minor triad with added major seventh) moving in parallel. There is the gradual addition of bird-like figures in the solo first violin produced by high artificial harmonics with glissandos; a solo second violin shadows these with wide-ranging sextuplets. The solo viola recalls the alternating fifths of the second section in the final crescendo; the recorder's final long note is shattered by the inevitable effects of the instruction to overblow.

Michael Smetanin and the Majestic Clockwork

It wasn't exactly your *Rite of Spring* type riot, but in 1988 Michael Smetanin gained more than 15 minutes of notoriety. Recently returned to Sydney after study with Louis Andriessen in the Netherlands, Smetanin had composed a new orchestral work commissioned by the ABC for the Melbourne Symphony Orchestra. *Black Snow* took its name from a story by Russian author Mikhail Bulgakov (best known in Anglophone countries for *The Master and Margarita*). Smetanin is of Russian heritage, but more importantly, Bulgakov's story – which satirises the Moscow-based avant-garde of the 1930s – touched a chord with Smetanin who felt at the time that many of his colleagues had sold out in a bid for popularity and success. In the event the scheduled performance was cancelled: the conductor had fallen ill, the orchestra was due to leave for an international tour two days later, the saxophone parts were incorrectly copied. So the Sydney Symphony Orchestra was prevailed upon to premiere the work – in the face of some intense opposition from some players – and did so, gaining the composer some of the most extensive coverage of his career to date. The music was very, very loud and gave the impression of a composer happily making obscene gestures at the musical establishment. It was also very, very good.

Smetanin had initially studied at the Sydney Conservatorium under Richard Toop, the British-born musicologist who had been an assistant teacher to the late Karlheinz Stockhausen in Cologne before settling in Sydney in the mid-1970s. Toop encouraged Smetanin, and student colleagues like Gerard Brophy and Elena Kats-Chernin, to pursue what we might call high modernism in their work, very much attuned to contemporary developments in European music. Smetanin's earliest music, then, brought together three strands. The first of these is the vanguard modernism of Stockhausen which has two relevant aspects here: aesthetically, the European avant-garde had a political program (derived in part from the works of philosophers like Theodor Adorno[4]) that insisted on the need for a clean slate with each new work, in large part a response to the implication of high culture in the crimes of World War II. Related to this is the structural principle that Stockhausen developed in the early 1960s which he called 'moment form'; eschewing development and traditional large-scale structures, moment form treats each successive moment as a unique object of contemplation.

The second strand is the peculiarly Dutch take on minimalism pioneered by Andriessen and others. Unlike the seamless, polished edge of the music of Glass or Reich, Andriessen's music combines insistent repetitive structures with a more abrasive approach to harmony and timbre. This in itself sits comfortably with the third strand, Smetanin's early love of hard rock music – both for its sheer physicality as well as its culturally subversive pretensions.

So, with the cause célèbre of *Black Snow*, all the elements were in place for Smetanin to attract the reputation of 'bad boy of Australian music' – one that in subsequent years he fostered to some extent. In the later 1980s and 1990s, for instance, he like many colleagues cultivated the suggestive-monosyllable-as-title in works like *Strip*, *Stroke* and *Spray*; the commercial recording of his song cycle *The Skinless Kiss of Angels* for soprano, baritone and ensemble enjoyed the notoriety of an obscenity warning-sticker on its front cover. Two decades on, the reputation is unhelpful to say the least, given that Smetanin now enjoys a career teaching composition at the Sydney Conservatorium and that his music has, inevitably, changed.

The change has been one of emphasis rather than style. The suggestive-monosyllable pieces remain fine works, as are those written during Smetanin's 1988 residency with Musica Viva Australia, the string quartet *Red Lightning* and larger ensemble work *Fylgir* among them. *The Skinless Kiss of Angels* (1992) paved the way for two significant chamber operas, *The Burrow* (1993), a dramatisation of the last moments of Franz Kafka's life, and *Gauguin* (2000), both to librettos by poet Alison Croggon. *Strip*, for string orchestra (composed for the Australian Chamber Orchestra), took a cue from Andriessen's *Symphony for Open Strings*; using only open strings and natural harmonics (with instruments variously tuned to provide a wide spectrum of available pitch) creates a mercurial shimmering texture like the refraction of light in mist. *Stroke*, a satellite work of *Black Snow*, is a thrilling nine-minute piano solo that encapsulates many of Smetanin's musical concerns of the time: the emphatic rhythmic and harmonic rhetoric, and what Richard Toop, in an analysis of the work, has described as its 'kaleidoscopic' form.

In the wake of *Black Snow*, which, on several occasions, Smetanin has described as being 'intuitively' written, the composer began experimenting with pre-compositional strategies to enhance the form of his music. In the ensemble piece *Strange Attractions* (1990) Smetanin explored some of the implications of chaos theory after reading Stephen Hawking's *A Brief History of Time*: following Hawking's terminology, Smetanin developed what he called the 'cellular automaton', in which a set of relationships between musical elements such as pitch were established before composition commenced. The objection that this circumscribes the composer's intuition and spontaneity is both obvious and wrong: in any system, be it diatonic harmony, twelve-note serialism or the Indian *raga*, certain procedures are automatically impossible. Moreover, as Smetanin has noted, a composer like Messiaen didn't slavishly restrict himself to his modes of limited transposition if the creative context demanded otherwise. The automaton merely helps to generate patterns which the composer then manipulates at will. Smetanin's harmony is emphatically non-diatonic but the logical integrity of his music is perfectly audible.

Stroke was composed for the New York-based Australian pianist Lisa Moore, who has also championed the work of Elena Kats-Chernin, Gerard Brophy and Andrew Ford. Smetanin's piano concerto *Mysterium cosmographicum* was premiered by Moore with the Sydney Symphony Orchestra in 2005. The title ('The Cosmographic Mystery') is that of the first major work of astronomy published by Johannes Kepler (and also the subtitle, incidentally, of Larry Sitsky's 1971 Concerto for Violin, Orchestra and Female Voices). Kepler's book, published in 1596, sought to prove the validity of Copernicus' theory that the planets all revolve around the sun, and to harmonise that system with Christian theology. Put simply, Kepler proposed that the five Platonic solids could nest with a sphere drawn around the outer points of each, one inside the other, with the simplest, the tetrahedron, at the core. The six spheres thus created would represent the orbit of the known planets. In his program note on the piano concerto, Smetanin points out that:

> central to the structure of this 22-minute piano concerto is the idea of musical shapes within shapes. A technical approach that I have often used, here it is a reflection of the Kepler model. The piece doesn't make exact use of Kepler's numbers and ratios, as their complexity and size were not useful to my work.[5]

Smetanin also goes on to say that in the final section of Kepler's 1619 *Harmonices Mundi* ('The harmony of the worlds'):

Kepler generates diatonic scales and other musical figures by juxtaposing ratios from celestial movements in our galaxy. The most interesting of those I found were the up and down (triangular) scalar figures he derived to represent the planets and our moon. These figures formed the basis of my decision to feature triangular shapes in the structure of this work at a number of levels, down to the smallest melodic units.

Smetanin also used two series of numbers, where each new number is the sum of the two previous, to generate some material: the Fibonacci series (1, 2, 3, 5, 8 and so on), and the Lucas series (1, 3, 4, 7, 11 ...). As the composer notes, the sum of pairs of Fibonacci numbers that are separated by one other, such as 2+5 or 3+8, always yield a Lucas number. Thus the two series effectively nest inside one another in the same way as Kepler's Platonic shapes. This translates into musical material by the simple use of the numbers to define degrees of the scale: in diatonic harmony the Fibonacci numbers 1, 3, 5, 8 give us the common triad (plus octave); in a chromatic scale starting on A we would end up with A, C, D, F. Thus Smetanin can use the number series to generate pitch patterns which can be used as melody or harmony and which act as points of reference in the unfolding of any given work.

Smetanin's concerto plays for a little over twenty minutes, and immediately establishes a sense of the 'majestic clockwork' with a scattering of bright, high sounds from what Smetanin calls the 'continuo' instrumental group: solo piano, orchestral piano and three percussionists. Against a quietly insistent hammering of chords from the orchestral piano (whose repeated right-hand minor seventh will have great structural importance), triangular shapes are in evidence immediately. The Chinese bell tree has a down/up/down contour mirrored in the crotales and solo piano; the timpani enter subsequently with a narrow up/down glissando over two bars. The entire first section of the work is given over to the continuo group and its chiming. Smetanin avoids monotony by the discreet use of 'short' bars – $\frac{3}{4}$, $\frac{3}{8}$, $\frac{5}{16}$ – against the prevailing $\frac{4}{4}$ pulse. These shorter bars invariably announce a change of tonal emphasis on the following downbeat. The prevailing tessitura is high (the bass is provided by the somewhat recessive five-octave marimba and timpani), but lower notes start to appear in the solo part signalling a new section. Here the tempo is slower (down to 64 bpm from 80) and the metre predominantly $\frac{3}{4}$. Where the piano parts were chordal, here they are more monodic, dovetailing subtly between instruments. The cellos announce a rising and falling glissando over a minor seventh – another triangular shape; the violins hold notes a minor seventh apart as a pedal point. Against this, trios of woodwinds play a gentle pulse of semiquavers, moving gradually up quarter-tone scales to create a blurred effect; these and the string glissandos provide contrast to the fixed hard-edged sounds of the pianos and percussion.

A third, slower section starts with solo piano alone, playing figurations that cover a wider compass and contain more rhythmic differentiation. There is a brief reminiscence of the opening as the second piano joins the soloist: the latter's florid scale passages are underpinned by rapid repeated notes in the former's line. More aggressive quintuplet figures emerge, leading to a new section of 64 bpm. Here the first violins' D-E flat-D motif provides the triangular contour; the solo piano's semiquavers are offset by accents on every fifth note as the blurring quarter-tone scales recur in the winds. A peremptory blast of trumpets masks the beginning of a short digression with long high lines in harmonics from the strings, against wide sextuplet passagework in the solo part. The wind lines become more urgent, as the pianos' unison lines (Smetanin, like Debussy, knows the dramatic value of two pianos in unison) describe wider triangular shapes.

The continuo group interrupts with a barrage of triplets, the solo piano part full of bright fourths and octaves, and this proceeds in a call and response with flutes, who create an eerie texture of tremolando, 'out of tune' harmonics. Under this is a series of slow, narrow glissandos in the violas that in turn gives way to an aggressive up/down glissando pattern – outlining a minor seventh – in the first violins. This ostinato is punctuated by short loud chords from winds and keyboards, or dying falls of triplet quarter-tones. Tension builds with angular quaver figures from the continuo, sinister snarls from tuba and the ascent of the violins to the very top of their compass. The music picks up speed, first with hammering triplets throughout the orchestra at 96 bpm then, over obsessively sliding sevenths in the lower strings, emphatically loud passagework in piano and winds leads into a glittering solo cadenza.

The reminiscence of the work's opening at the end of the cadenza is almost shockingly classical, but this is of course no literal recapitulation. In fact the relentlessness of the opening gesture is now interrupted by empty bars, allowing the sonorities of the continuo group to fade into silence before a return to the monodic piano writing and blurred wind figurations of the work's second section. This gives rise to some rare solo writing for winds, soon subsumed by more homophonic textures that are themselves overcome by big gestures from the solo piano. There is a further memory of the work's opening gestures with short stabbing chords from the brass and a gradual deliquescence. A short, extremely quiet passage for strings introduces the piano's last virtuosic display below triangulating glissandos. In the work's final moments, a gentle glinting of semiquavers from pianos and Chinese bells echoes and fades into the far distance. It's as if we have glimpsed part of an eternally ongoing process.

Carl Vine: How Can We Know the Dancer from the Dance?

In 1992 the Sydney Dance Company's artistic director, Graeme Murphy, presented one of his best shows. No silly frocks, protecting veils or over-produced sound effects – not even, mercifully, a story: just beautiful, exuberant ensemble dancing with an added frisson of danger from a deliberately low-slung, swinging lighting rig. Murphy had, and it's greatly to his credit, commissioned the score for this piece – indeed he had a good track record of commissioning and featuring new Australian music for the company. This time it was Carl Vine's first Piano Sonata, and as the dancers did their stuff on stage, so too did pianist Michael Kieran Harvey. The combined effect of virtuosic dancing and musical performance was electrifying; so was the music itself.

Born in 1954, Vine is of a generation that was coming to maturity as many of its older colleagues were questioning the nostrums of contemporary music. Still, as the student of John Exton at the University of Western Australia, Vine was raised on a strictly serial diet – his early *Miniature II* for two violas written as a student in the 1970s reflects Exton's interest in the musical language of Webern in its spare aphoristic style. While Vine would in due course embrace what he has called a 'radically tonal' idiom, the lessons of concision and poise were well learned. It was in the 1970s too that Vine formed a relationship which would have far-reaching effects on his music: in 1976 he met Murphy, who commissioned Vine to compose the score for his 1978 work, *Poppy*, based on the life of Jean Cocteau. In 1976 Murphy became artistic director of The Dance Company (NSW) which in 1979 became the Sydney Dance Company.

The year 1979 also saw the foundation of Flederman, the contemporary music ensemble which included composer and clarinettist Nigel Westlake, flautist Geoffrey Collins, percussionist Graeme Leak, trombonist Simone de Haan and Vine on piano. Vine's *Miniature III* (1983) is a showpiece for those performers, and inaugurates a series of chamber works for Flederman, Synergy and the Australia Ensemble. The *Knips Suite*, composed for London dance company Spink Inc in 1979, is also Vine's first string quartet and displays his keen ear for musical parody. To date he has produced five quartets making him probably the most prolific living Australian writer in that genre after Felix Werder and Peter Sculthorpe.

Piano Sonata – Sydney Dance Company in Graeme Murphy's choreography to Carl Vine's Piano Sonata No. 1, 1992. Photo by Branco Gaica.

Parallel to his interest in the 'standard' string quartet – in contrast to the mixed-instrument ensemble – is Vine's emergence as the most prolific symphonist (after Alfred Hill) in this country, with seven such works to his credit. His first, the *MicroSymphony*, dates from 1986 and is a short but concentrated work which establishes a number of hallmarks of Vine's mature style: a use of tonal or diatonic harmony

with a distinctive flavour, orchestration in which melody is thrown into high relief by the use of doubling at the octave, a fondness for powerful rhythmic ostinatos which gather strength as they go (like his colleague, Graeme Koehne's, Vine's experience of dance remains an important presence in his concert works) and a precisely judged use of sudden change from one section to another. In 1986 Vine had also composed *Love Song*, for trombone and tape, in which he forswore dogmatic modernism and developed a new style based on a rethinking of traditional melody and diatonic harmony.

The first three symphonies are structured on the principles of the elaboration of limited thematic elements and the synthesis of contrasting material; they are all highly affirmative works, as we hear in the wonderful big finish of the Third. The original version of the Fourth, by contrast, explored the drama which results when traditional notions of symphonic form are undermined, while the Fifth, or *Percussion Symphony*, puts the percussion section through its paces at the front of the stage for a change. Vine has generally avoided any sense of his concert music's being anything other than 'absolute' in intent, though in the *Choral Symphony* it goes without saying that in choosing liturgical texts (even in a very dead language) the music has some commentary function. The Seventh Symphony is subtitled 'scenes from daily life' though the six sections 'depict no explicit, predetermined images, actions or events. They remain abstract emblems of the drama of human interaction on a human scale within a readily identifiable musical vocabulary'. Nonetheless, in his program note Vine also refers to the 'incessant daily onslaught of violent and confronting images ... until recently nobody was able to appreciate the global scale of decimation and desolation wrought every day by our global family and, in the final analysis, by each one of ourselves'.[6]

Vine wrote his Piano Sonata No. 1 in 1990 and its first performance took place in Melbourne in 1991, a year before the Sydney Dance show. The work is thus roughly contemporary with the Third Symphony and shares its contrasts of big moments and more intimate, introspective ones. Unlike the Third Symphony, the sonata is in two separate movements, though there are certain thematic correspondences between them. Vine's model for the sonata was that of the US composer Elliott Carter. Carter's Piano Sonata, composed in 1945–46, is also in two movements, contains a similarly dramatic use of contrast between music of different tempos and uses a richly extended diatonic harmony. In his slightly earlier Cello Sonata, Carter explored a principle known as 'metrical modulation', which he developed in his piano sonata and which Carl Vine has used to great effect in numerous works. In harmony, a modulation is a way of smoothly changing key via a 'pivot chord', a chord common to both the old and new keys. In metrical (or tempo) modulation an analogous thing happens: a cross rhythm in the old section is used to establish a new speed. In this example we can see how the triplets in the old section become the basic pulse of the new one:

The effect is like changing gears — there's no slowing down or speeding up; we're suddenly in a new tempo.

Vine exploits this technique to breathtaking effect; indeed, he notes sternly in the preface to the score that the tempo markings 'are not suggestions but indications of absolute speed'. This is not just about the need to coordinate with intricate choreography. Strict adherence to Vine's tempo markings make the transitions thrilling, and the relative proportions of the different sections seem, as they should, inevitable.

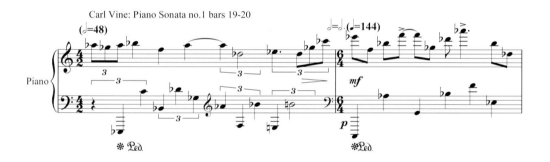

Carl Vine: Piano Sonata No. 1, bars 19–20. A classic instance of metrical modulation: note how the triplets in the first bar become the pulse of the following one. Used by permission of Chester Music (Music Sales Group).

The work's opening is a slow procession of six-note chords made up of stacked perfect fourths over a deep, open-fifth pedal. It is static and mysterious, but those triplets in the left hand give a sense of the latent energy which comes increasingly to the fore. As the movement progresses so the tempos become faster, with the music occasionally

Pianist Michael Kieran Harvey, dedicatee and first performer of Carl Vine's Piano Sonata No. 1. Photo by Bridget Elliot.

falling in a heap after a huge upward glissando. The first time this happens the music has new, pugnacious strength with terse punchy figures in the lower registers. The second time, the music returns to the very slow tempo of the opening, the music now decorated ornately as the movement comes to a close. The second movement is, as Vine puts it, a *moto perpetuo* which occasionally gives way to chorale-like figures with bright open fifths (a dilation of the fourths of the opening) in the right hand. These two elements are eventually combined, before the music returns to the very opening gesture and fades on the glint of a high major third.

This is music by someone who knows the instrument inside out, and who knows the precise strengths and sound of Michael Kieran Harvey, the soloist for whom it and several subsequent works were written.

Chapter 11

Myths and Legends, Ghosts and Monsters

The musics of Aboriginal Australia, Bali or ancient Japan all have their roots in ritual, acting out, reflecting on or embodying the archetypal stories that any culture tells itself over and over again. The mythology of pre-Christian Europe − that of ancient Greece in particular, though not exclusively − has had an abiding fascination for western artists, and forms part of the rich mix that inspires some Australian composers.

The 'mythic' invests music in a number of ways, from the abstract to the programmatic. In *A plaint for lost worlds*, Helen Gifford (born 1935) has composed a moving 'lament for jungles long ago, damaged stratosphere ... mourning the loss and belief in an innocent world of wonder and delight'.[1] This trio for piccolo, clarinet and piano is no more specific in its program, but Gifford − a composer who has worked chiefly in music for spoken-word theatre – creates an eloquent, word-less elegy. A number of recent works by Elena Kats-Chernin are based on fairytales; her orchestral *Mythic* is an abstracted distillation of some of those ideas. Brett Dean's *Amphitheatre* reflects on a now disused arte-fact, while Mary Finsterer evokes the Greek goddess of night in *Nyx*. *Ganymede/Prometheus* for instrumental quartet by Graham Hair (born 1943) is an excitingly intricate representation of two Greek myths as filtered through the poetry of Goethe. Gerard Brophy memorialised a friend in his string-orchestral *Orfeo*, referring to the mythic musician who 'made trees and the mountain-tops that freeze bow their heads when he did sing'.[2] Andrew Ford has visited the myth of Icarus – the boy who is given wings but flies too close to the sun – in two pieces: *Like Icarus Ascending* for solo violin and *Icarus Drowning* for mixed ensemble. In the former, Icarus' attempts to take flight represent the composer's attempts to get the piece off the ground, and that process becomes the argument of the piece.

As you might expect, though, myth is attractive to composers of vocal music: we have mentioned Carl Vine's *Choral Symphony* with its Akkadian invocations; Graham Hair's *Songs of the Sibyls* – prophetesses of the classical world – for three female voices and mixed ensemble is a masterpiece. And myth is especially attractive to composers for the stage. Opera as we know it was, in part, invented by Italian composers seeking to recreate the stagecraft of ancient Greece, where tragedy was chanted in the amphitheatres. Classical myths formed the almost exclu-sive basis for librettos until the late eighteenth century; it made a huge comeback in the works of Wagner and has continued as an important stream in the twentieth and twenty-first centuries, where the mythic, thanks to Freud and Jung, is seen as powerfully representative of the human subconscious.

Australian composers who have brought classical myth to the stage include Peggy Glanville-Hicks, notably in *Nausicaa* (1960) – based on the novel *Homer's Daughter* by Robert Graves, which explores the theory of Samuel Butler that the *Odyssey* was in fact written by a woman – and *Sappho* (1963) to a libretto by Lawrence Durrell. Much more recently there have been major mythical works from Liza Lim, whose 1993 *Oresteia*, a collaboration with Barrie Kosky, she describes as 'memory opera'; in 2008 Lim's *The Navigator*, which draws on elements from Celtic mythology and the Indian epic *Mahabharata*, premiered in Brisbane. Elena Kats-Chernin's take on the classics in *Iphis* was inevitably wacky, a genuinely funny version of this Ovidian tale of sexual transformation. Richard Mills' third major opera, *The Love of the Nightingale* (2007), also uses a story found in Ovid's *Metamorphosis*, though unlike *Iphis* this is violent and tragic.

Larry Sitsky's major work in this vein is *The Golem*, based on a version of the ancient Jewish legend of the man created out of clay by a rabbi to protect his embattled people. This version, which the great Australian poet Gwen Harwood fashioned into an exemplary libretto, is set in 16th century Prague where Rabbi Judah Loew is persuaded by two sorcerers that it would be possible to create such a being. He does so, creating a man from clay and fixing a holy seal on his forehead. The Golem protects the Jews from Christian thugs who want to frame them for ritual sacrifice (the famous 'blood libel') and murder but he and Rachel, the Rabbi's daughter, fall in love. This arouses the intense jealousy of a gypsy servant, who contrives to get the Golem drunk; this in turn leads to a further attack by the Christians in which Rachel is killed. The Golem attacks blindly, killing Christians and Jews, so the Rabbi regretfully removes the holy seal, and with it the Golem's life. It is full-scale grand opera, genuinely tragic, and in it Sitsky has exploited a range of musical gambits from the tender to the acerbically expressionistic.

Scene from the Australian Opera's world premiere production of *The Golem* (1993), composed by Larry Sitsky, libretto by Gwen Harwood, directed by Barrie Kosky, designed by Michael AR Anderson (sets and costumes) and Nigel Levings (lighting). Patrick Togher as Isaac, Kerry Henderson as The Golem, Lindsay Gaffney as Jacob. Photo by Kiren Chang.

As the curtain rises on *Madeline Lee* (2004), composed by John Haddock (born 1957) to a libretto by him and Michael Campbell, we enter a world not immediately identifiable as mythical. Beside a plane

that has crashed in a desert, a group of young men are playing baseball, showing off, putting each other down and fantasising about their
team's mascot, a girl in the stadium crowd called Madeline Lee. The
plane is a US Airforce B-17 Flying Fortress, nicknamed *Madeline Lee*,
and the men are its crew. They appear to have survived the crash and
are waiting on their absent captain's orders for the rescue mission. A
mission does arrive, led by the Major who turns out to be the Captain
in command of the plane. The young men approach him, and it is
only then we realise they are the ghosts of the crew. The Captain, as

Composer John Haddock (left) and librettist/director Michael Campbell on the set of *Madeline Lee*. Photo by Bridget Elliot.

he then was, had bailed out and survived, telling his superiors that all the crew had done likewise; it is now twenty years later, and his First Officer on the rescue mission suspects that all is not as it seems. The Major, finding a talismanic baseball glove in the sand, must now face his memories, his abandonment of his crew – especially a wounded crew member known as The Boy – and his deception: his aria 'I have hung twenty years between Madeline Lee and the sea' is the emotional climax of the work, where he attempts to shoot himself and the ghost-crew saves him. Only now can he and they find peace. The work is at one level, then, a parable of guilt and expiation – the stuff of myth. Haddock's music is cast in an uncomplicated diatonic style; many years' experience on the staff of Opera Australia has given him a fine sense of idiomatic writing for the voice and an inside knowledge of how to use a pit orchestra. Comparisons with Benjamin Britten – especially *Billy Budd*, another all-male opera – are inevitable and valid, but not odious. Haddock is not afraid of a big tune, or a big moment, but also uses deft touches such as the combination of high, wailing bassoon and celesta. The music is extremely powerful when the Major starts to relive the plane's last flight, giving a real sense of the noise, speed and chaos.

In the next sections we will examine how Elena Kats-Chernin and Richard Mills 'translate' myth into music for both concert hall and stage.

Elena Kats-Chernin and the Eternal Return

At a concert in 1995, the sadly now defunct Sydney Alpha Ensemble performed its usual spread of new work. Among the local offerings was a heartfelt and earnest work by a composer and academic that warned of the perils of environmental degradation, followed by a piece from a composer who had recently made the brave decision to return from Europe with three small children in tow and, at that point, a tenuous freelance career. In a reminder that the quality of art has only a tangential relationship to its creator's biography, the work, *Cadences*,

Deviations and Scarlatti for fourteen instruments was joyful, witty and wholly engrossing; the composer was Elena Kats-Chernin.

Kats-Chernin has enjoyed international recognition in recent years through such high-profile projects as her composition for the opening ceremony of the Sydney Olympics in 2000. At the same time she is a composer-pianist, producing a high volume of small-scale solo piano work to perform herself. She has written opera (including the mythic comedy *Iphis*, *Matricide* and *Undertow*), ballet (*Wild Swans*), numerous orchestral pieces including two piano concertos and a vast amount of music for solo instruments and smaller ensembles.

Kats-Chernin was born in Tashkent, capital of what is now the republic of Uzbekistan, but immigrated to Australia with her family in 1975. Between 1976 and 1979 she studied composition at the Sydney Conservatorium with Richard Toop, and in 1980 travelled to Germany for further study with Helmut Lachenmann, a composer whose interest in the fundamental nature – the 'anatomy', as he puts it – of sound has generated works of great individuality. Toop and Lachenmann gave Kats-Chernin an impressive modernist pedigree, reflected in early works like *In Tension* (which also displays her love of the off-beat punning title). *In Tension* dates from 1982 and is scored for flute, clarinet, percussion, piano, violin and cello. It is of course an early work, and not surprisingly bears some of the hallmarks of German modernism: its opening textures, for instance, are built from a combination of motoric scale passages and terse, isolated gestures; the harmony is freely non-diatonic. There is a Lachenmann-esque use of unconventional instrumental sounds, there are extremes of range and dynamics, and passages where the instrumental lines seem blissfully unaware of each other.

The piece is also genuinely funny, a virtue we should not take for granted. And it is funny not because it is attempting to parody itself or its models – it isn't – but because the composer has an impeccable sense of timing for the unexpected sound or gesture, and the material never outstays its welcome. Even in what is essentially a student piece, the comic sensibility that distinguishes Kats-Chernin's work is

Elena Kats-Chernin at the keyboard. Photo by Bridget Elliot.

in evidence. By comic I don't mean constantly laugh-out-loud funny, though in the sometimes uptight, po-faced world of contemporary music it is refreshing to be able to do so: a rippling dominant seventh arpeggio, the parlour-pianist's equivalent of musical throat-clearing, is the *last* thing we hear in her marvellous piano piece *Tast-En* (after a passage of chordal writing which is extremely beautiful); her affection-ate relationship to Bach in her recorder concerto *Re-inventions* or her recent String Quartet, *From the Notebook of Anna Magdalena Bach*, or indeed Scarlatti in *Cadences, Deviations and Scarlatti*, never precludes humour.

In the mid-1970s, Lachenmann departed from one of the key modern-ist orthodoxies by introducing references to pre-existing music, such as the Mozart Clarinet Concerto, into his own. (The Stockhausen/Boulez generation preferred to think of every new piece as being unique, and drawn on a clean slate.) Kats-Chernin's music from the mid-1990s has a similar relationship with the music of the past with one crucial differ-ence. In 1993 she produced two important pieces: *Clocks*, for Ensemble Modern, which she describes as her breakthrough work; and a short orchestral piece, *Retonica*, whose neologistic title – derived from 'return-ing to the tonic' – says much. In classical sonata design a 'return to the tonic' signifies a recapitulation; here it also describes Kats-Chernin's embracing diatonic harmony. In this, of course, she is not alone, and like a number of her colleagues has, as part of this rapprochement with the diatonic system, also explored the use of certain forms from popular music and often crossbred them with aspects of other musi-cal traditions. Pieces like *Schubert Blues*, which extracts and varies harmonic material from that composer's 'Death and the Maiden', or her celebrated *Russian Rag* are examples. In the hugely entertaining *Iphis* of 1997 (based on Ovid's tale of sexual metamorphosis) there's the occasional whiff of Bayreuth, some feral kletzmer and more than a hint of old Berlin. The music ranges from rancid to radiant, and is occasionally unashamedly cheesy, but always hits its dramatic target.

Late in the 1990s the Tasmanian Symphony Orchestra commis-sioned an orchestral work called *Heaven is Closed* which proved to be quintessential Kats-Chernin. Relentlessly energetic, the piece has a manic, cartoonish feel; as David Garrett pointed out in his annotation to the work, when Kats-Chernin 'thinks about heaven, the idea of blissful states and places often visits her in vivid images of the picture-book fairy stories of Russian childhood. Folk imagination portrays heaven as a playful place ....'.[3] It is perhaps at this time that a certain Russian quality starts to surface in Kats-Chernin's work, though *Russian Rag*'s first incarnation is 1996. In these works there is the rhythmic emphasis of Stravinsky, and a Romantic melancholy (that nonetheless never descends into self-pity) that we might associate with late-nineteenth-century Russian music. And there is the sense of irony which for Kats-Chernin has not been forced by circumstance into the sardonic bitterness of Shostakovich.

As Garrett suggests, Kats-Chernin's Russianness is tied up with picture-book fairy stories, and these have played an increasing role in her work since the late 1990s. Recent works in this vein include *Wild Swans*, a full-length ballet based on a fairy story by Hans Christian Andersen. The story's heroine, Eliza, suffers at the hands of her evil stepmother who turns her eleven brothers into swans. To break the spell Eliza must knit coats for the swans out of stinging nettles while never uttering a word, during which time she meets and marries the Prince and is suspected by the locals of being a witch. (Kats-Chernin's response to Eliza's silence is to add a soprano, singing *vocalise*, to the orchestra.) The score is unsurprisingly eclectic, referring, however obliquely, to Prokofiev and Stravinsky, American minimalism and Messiaen at his most sci-fi soundtrack-like, all the while responding adroitly to the demands of the drama.

The fairytale ballet is something of a Russian specialty; more recently Kats-Chernin has used Russian fairytales in concert music such as her Piano Trio *The Spirit and the Maiden* (which exists in versions with and without soprano voice). When she was commissioned to write a new piece for the Tasmanian Symphony Orchestra in 2004, Kats-Chernin wanted to write something very different in tone and mood from *Heaven is Closed*. The result was the twelve-minute work, *Mythic*, where the composer explores, initially at least, music which is relatively calm on the surface but concealing a genuine and moving pathos. As Kats-Chernin explains:

> I wanted to attempt a direction I had not explored previously, and that was to stay in a slow, dark mood for a lengthy period and to see where that took me. Eventually it grew into a kind of a hymn with variations, sometimes almost Romantic, that made extensive use of the Orchestra's brass section. The title *Mythic* refers to the mental image I had of musically entering into a large, mythical cave.[4]

As in works like *Chamber of Horrors* for harp or *Hemispheres* for London's Nash Ensemble, *Mythic* draws its material from the repetition and elaboration of what Kats-Chernin has described as 'a passacaglia-like chordal progression which had grabbed hold of me and wouldn't let go'. The simplicity of the material is announced right at the start where the double bass and cellos are divided to produce a slow-moving homophonic texture in four parts and in common time. (See music example.) The two lowest parts move in parallel fifths, giving a sense of space and resonance, and conjuring, perhaps, medieval organum or Slavonic chant. The string chords are essentially diatonic, but right from the first beat, Kats-Chernin compromises any sense of tonal safety with the first of several (magical?) harp chords: here the D minor-ish strings are haloed by the harp's essentially B flat minor chord. So by stealth almost, Kats-Chernin begins with a pungent but subtle dissonance (the resulting chord contains six different pitches, with the interval of the semitone prominent in the mix); the bitonal implications reverberate throughout the piece. Even this abstract 'myth' contains the hallmarks of danger, ambiguity and transformation.

Having established the harmonic engine of the piece, Kats-Chernin brings in a simple melody for violas with the instruction to play *sul tasto*: bowing above the fingerboard produces a wan sound, made more desolate by the instruction to play with little vibrato. This has all been by way of introduction, as the full string band, still low in its compass, now enters with a characteristic rhythm (short-short-long, or minim-

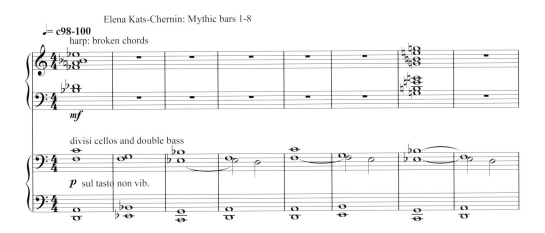

Elena Kats-Chernin: *Mythic*, bars 1–8. Notice how the harp adds bitonal dissonance to the otherwise simple 'chorale'. Used by permission of Boosey and Hawkes.

minim-semibreve) in which we hear the melodic contour which dominates the whole piece. It has several versions, ranging from tightly chromatic to diatonically stable; here it is diatonic, with harmony that includes emotive suspensions on the strong beats. Flutes and then clarinets, using flutter-tongue, join the string texture before reverting to more traditional figures, such as punctuating scale motifs. The piece has a tremendous sense of latent energy, which Kats-Chernin effects by slightly ratcheting up the tempo at each new version of the material. And in each new section, different parts of the orchestra come to the foreground: over the strings' melodic statements, the woodwinds, for instance, go on to provide angular bitonal interjections which become more ornate and importunate before yielding to a section in which the arch-Romantic French horn takes over the thematic weight. Against the horn's long melody, other brass instruments tap out a version of the short-short-long motif now much faster and martial. Sure enough, the next section is a kind of march, with the brass carrying the theme and the strings and winds providing crisp syncopations – made crisper by the exploitation of the bitonal relationship set up at the start.

Kats-Chernin has so far been building up the textures and gradually increasing the speed of the work, but pulls back for a lightly scored section in which the tenor trombone solo has the melody accompanied by angular violin and harp writing. From here the momentum and tension builds again, culminating in a statement of the theme from the full orchestra in an unambiguous C minor. Just when you thought the music had reached a state of fully diatonic stability, however, Kats-Chernin introduces the first of several disruptive elements: the winds maintain the simple diatonic harmony but at odds with that of the strings. And the vibraphone player is instructed to strike the keys with claves, thus creating cluster harmonies and a metallic racket that could be some mythic creature coming to life. Then, in the following section, the so-far stable $\frac{4}{4}$ metre starts to admit $\frac{3}{4}$ bars, throwing the tread of the music off balance. This issues in a passage of $\frac{5}{4}$, where the combination of the recognisable harmonic progression and irregular metres creates huge tension; the occasional $\frac{6}{4}$ bar appears, offering some fleeting waltz rhythms before the music peters out into the quiet white-noise sound of shimmering violas (playing *sul ponticello*, or close to the bridge) and deliberately inexpressive lines from solo winds.

It is as if the music has reached a point of exhaustion, with the gradual addition of more glacially cold sounds. There is some respite in the final coda of the piece. The strings are divided across the range of the section producing an unexpected quiet lushness; this is taken up by gently fluttering winds. Chords from strings and harp make an arresting sound, as the harp's 'broken' figuration is echoed by the reiterating bounce of the *saltando* (jumping) bows. A passage of simple homophony, largely for strings though with the harp characteristically adding 'wrong' chords, leads to a quiet, not quite resolved, close.

There is no 'story' to *Mythic*, though the use of harp and French horn at various points has a clear lineage in the fairytale works of any number of Russian composers, particularly the Tchaikovsky of *The Nutcracker*. Like them, Kats-Chernin is a master at creating momentum with minimal information. Active textures, ostinatos and other repetitions give this music an unfaltering headlong motion; her innate sense of drama knows just when to throw that motion off balance. The effect of the work is of experiencing something half familiar, half strange, a transformation after which there will be no return.

Richard Mills: Philomel with Melody

Musicologist Robert Donington wrote extensively on opera, particularly Wagner, from a Jungian perspective.[5] He believed that the presence of music dispelled any sense of naturalism in the drama being presented, and that therefore it was an ideal medium for the presentation of archetypes or universal symbols, rather than the rational examination of individual character. If we accept this, and it makes much sense, opera is very close to myth, and as we know, composers from the time of Monteverdi through to our own have been fascinated with mythological subjects. This is not to say it must always be about gods and heroes; Verdi, Puccini and Britten, to name but three, found the mythic resonances in much more recent stories.

In his three full-scale operas, Richard Mills has essayed the mythic, but most explicitly in *The Love of the Nightingale*, composed to a libretto by Timberlake Wertenbaker based on a story from Ovid's *Metamorphoses*. Ovid was a 'poet about town' in the time of Augustus Caesar – until some undisclosed insult or indiscretion caused him to be banished from Rome to the shores of the Black Sea, where he composed his *Tristia* and *Black Sea Letters*. In Rome, however, he was known as the poet of the *Amores* and *Ars amatoria*, both urbane and witty takes on love, and the *Metamorphoses*, a compendium of stories beginning with the creation of the world and ending with the glories of Rome, all linked by the theme of transformation where humans are changed into animals or trees, statues come to life and gods change their form.

In Book 6 of *Metamorphoses* Ovid tells the story of Philomela. When Athens is saved from barbarian invasion by Tereus, King of Thrace, Pandion, the Athenian King, promises his elder daughter Procne in marriage. After some years Procne asks if her sister Philomela might be allowed to visit her in her new home; Tereus returns to Athens to collect Philomela, and is seized by lust for her. They return to Thrace, where he locks her in a lonely tower and rapes her. Philomela threatens to fill the forest with her cries, and Tereus cuts out her tongue. Philomela manages to weave a garment with images of her story and smuggle it to the palace. Procne rescues and disguises her and takes her to the palace. On the feast of Bacchus she murders her own son, Itys, and feeds the flesh to his father, Tereus. Realising what has happened, Tereus attempts to kill Procne and Philomela. The gods intervene; Philomela is changed into a nightingale, Procne into a swallow, and Tereus into a hoopoe.

Opera is also perfect for sex and violence. Mills' *The Love of the Nightingale* is gripping in its depiction of slaughter and mutilation, tender where it evokes love, and radiant in the final scene where the characters, now changed utterly, reflect on their gruesome lives. The opera's opening scenes, for instance, juxtapose fearsome war music − dissonant and angular, with piled-up harmony in double chorus and orchestra, and martial tattoos from percussion − with the playful, loving music of the two sisters. Mills' music for Philomele (as she is called in this version[6]) straightaway identifies her as the 'girl full of laughter', her coloratura runs and trills adumbrating her later transformation. In Wertenbaker's account of the story, Procne finds herself miserable in the cold northern kingdom, and isolated from the society of the Thracian women. For their part they feel unable to communicate with her, ominously saying 'we do not have the words'. Procne demands to see Philomele, and Tereus, at this stage desperate to make Procne happy, returns to Athens. There, Pandion hosts a play that tells the story of Phaedra and Hippolytus, best known from Euripides' *Hippolytus*: Phaedra is the

Scene from *The Love of the Nightingale* by Richard Mills and Timberlake Wertenbaker. A Wesfarmers Arts Commission; a co-production of UWA Perth International Arts Festival, West Australian Opera, Queensland Music Festival, Opera Queensland, Queensland Performing Arts Centre and Victorian Opera. Anke Höppner as Procne with Women of Thrace. Photo by Rob Maccoll.

second wife of Theseus, whose son Hippolytus hates all women. In revenge, Aphrodite the goddess of love causes Phaedra to fall for her stepson; Phaedra's nurse tells the young man, whose scornful response causes Phaedra to hang herself in shame, which Theseus takes as a sign of guilt. He calls on Poseidon, god of the sea, to kill Hippolytus.

Here, in the opera, Tereus feels the touch of mighty Aphrodite; here he becomes hopelessly obsessed with Philomele. It is important to note that Tereus is presented as a sympathetic character at first – Mills gives him an attractive aria to prove it. This is not to excuse his behaviour but to point out that the growth of evil in him is what is dramatised here. The crux of this version of the story is the abuse of women by powerful men, and the attendant ruthlessness that causes Tereus to deceive – he tells Philomele that Procne has died, and tells Procne the same about her sister. And he kills his own Captain when the latter falls in love with Philomele.

In the second Act the violence latent in the first is intensified by an order of magnitude. Rebuffed by Philomele, Tereus rapes her with, it is later revealed, a sword – owing to his impotence. Philomele taunts him about that, in a bravura passage of coloratura recalling her laughter in Act I and presaging her nightingale voice. As her line becomes more and more extravagant, Tereus becomes more and more angry, and when Philomele reaches an ecstatic top E – three lines above the stave – he cuts out her tongue with the curt 'This will stop your words'. One of Wertenbaker's themes in this work is with the silencing of questions by power. The orchestra responds with a total-chromatic pile-up of dissonant chords.

In the Bacchic scene in which Itys is murdered by his mother, Mills makes full use of the ensemble of women's voices. In the Mills/Wertenbaker version Philomele tells her story by means of dolls she has made, rather than a woven garment, providing a structural balance with the Phaedra play. This takes place at the beginning of the Bacchic scene, where men and boys are forbidden in the palace. As Philomele plays out her story, the women, echoing their own lament in Act I, realise 'she has no words' and at that moment Procne recognises her sister, singing a tragic lament that 'this is what the world looks like'. Itys, egged on by two soldiers, is spying over a wall, interrupts the ritual and is sacrificed by the women. (Mills and Wertenbaker forego the cannibalism scene.) The chorus, as Tereus enters and realises what has happened, sets up a bloodcurdling cry of 'Justice, justice' to overlapped falling chromatic scales. Tereus' rage is captured in dense brass chords, frenetic drumming and one of several instances of recorded sound effects. The remaining characters, as chorus, explain how the metamorphosis has taken place.

There is then a radiant epilogue for Itys, Philomele, Procne and Tereus. Mills again uses aggregations of chords with different tonalities as in the response to the mutilation scene, but here the effect is like a photo negative. The effect is serene, melting, and it supports a short dialogue between Itys and Philomele, with Itys asking questions about why they had to change. In response the three adults sing a beautiful trio: 'we had to change' as 'the blood had to stop flowing, the anger to subside'. As an image of transformation, the music moves gently but constantly through different tonal centres, as it does in works like Britten's *A Midsummer Night's Dream* and Richard Strauss' *Metamorphosis* – each in its way a work about transformation. The questions having

Richard Mills: The Love of the Nightingale Act II scene 10 bars155-8

Richard Mills: *The Love of the Nightingale*, Act II scene 10, bars 155–58. Part of Philomele's final nightingale song. Used by permission of the composer.

been answered, Philomele brings the work to a close with an extended and beautiful coloratura vocalise.

Myth deals with the deep structures of our humanity and, in the case of this work, with issues of power, love and hate. It is thus a kind of parable of the need for radical transformation of the psyche or, if you will, the spirit. We will examine ways in which composers have explicitly explored questions of spirituality in the next section.

Chapter 12

The Place of Spirit

'Spirit' and 'spirituality' are words frequently found in the discussion of Australian music, especially those works which claim legitimacy from their relationships to Aboriginal or Asian culture, or to one or other of the many Australian landscapes. This is as it should be, even if there is a real danger of a shallow 'spirituality by association'. The use of a traditional melody or didjeridu sound can be far removed from an Aboriginal Australian's understanding of his or her relationship to a sacred site or ancestral 'dreamtime' story and the complex web of connection to others in the community, to their stories and sites. But as is demonstrated by such works as Liza Lim's *The Compass*, composers are becoming increasingly sensitive to this, and understanding that Aboriginal culture, like any other, is a dynamic and evolving thing, rather than a collection of sounds and gestures there to be dipped into in order to give the work national credibility. So it is with Asian-influenced works: composers are now less likely to see the concept of meditation merely as an excuse to write simple, slow music.

In as secular a society as modern Australia's, it is unsurprising that the word 'spirituality' conjures up images of scented candles, self-help manuals and foot massage – part of a privatised experience analogous to our consumption of music through the headphones of our MP3 player. There is no shortage of music in that vein being written here. In reality, though, spirituality in any tradition is about the individual's relationship to the community and the broader universe. While stressing the value of personal meditation, Buddhists also place enormous importance on the *sangka*, or community; communal prayer is part of the everyday life of the observant Muslim. And while the mainstream Christian churches have suffered a decline in regular membership, there are composers in this country whose work comes out of their relationship to two millennia or more of religious development. The work of the composers discussed in this section relates directly, though not necessarily uncritically, to the spiritual traditions of western religions. Some, like Claire McLean (born 1958) or Christopher Willcock (born 1947), work quite literally within a given tradition; others have used their cultural background as the basis for further exploration.

Of course, works with an overtly religious or spiritual program form a significant part of the western canon. Many, like Mozart's Requiem, were composed for liturgical use but found their way into concert programming; others, like Handel's *Messiah*, were always intended for the concert hall. Given the British nature of early Australian settlement, it's not surprising that the oratorio put down roots here: *Leichhardt's Grave*, the work in which Isaac Nathan prematurely mourned the German explorer in 1849, has its basis in that tradition, and Eugene Goossens' *The Apocalypse* just over a century later represents the extreme edge of it. Each Australian city has at least one well-established choral society (or heir thereof) and many of these have in recent years performed new work. Of course, choral music isn't necessarily 'spiritual', and spiritual music isn't necessarily vocal, but a number of contemporary composers have contributed music to the choral tradition which is grounded in traditional western spirituality. As we noted earlier, Peter Sculthorpe produced a full-scale Requiem in 2004, setting the liturgical text of the Mass for the Dead for solo didjeridu, choir and orchestra and blending an Aboriginal 'lullaby' into the texture. In 1998 we had the premiere of Anne Boyd's *Dreams for the Earth* to a text by senior students of Sydney's Abbotsleigh School (workshopped under the tutelage of Judith Rodriguez). The finest recent work for 'oratorio forces', however, is Nigel Butterley's *Spell of Creation*. This composer has always remained aloof from concerns about a national voice and the nature of Australian music's relationship to that of the rest of the world, instead quietly following his aesthetic concerns through to their logical conclusions. Much of his work is concerned with notions of transcendence, and throughout his career he has drawn together threads from a number of spiritual traditions to create a powerful personal syncretism. *Spell of Creation* is a summation of his life's work to date.

Larry Sitsky no longer professes any conventional faith, but, as he put it to Andrew Ford, has come to believe 'that music somehow can take us to a higher sphere ... I believe in the power of music to achieve these [mystical] states.'[1] Almost all of Sitsky's music has some mystical or metaphysical program; for instance, his four violin concertos reflect his interest in, respectively, the music of the spheres (*Mysterium cosmographicum*), theosophy (*Gurdjieff*), Chinese divination (*I Ching*) and, perhaps, Aboriginal cosmology (*Dreaming*). In the opera *The Golem*, Sitsky gives free rein to a number of these preoccupations.

Australian composers haven't written much liturgical Jewish music, although one post-war émigré, Werner Baer (1914–1992) composed significant works for the Great Synagogue in Sydney, and in the last few years Elena Kats-Chernin has done so for the Temple Emanuel in Woollahra. In the area of concert music, Mirrie Hill – wife of Alfred and in many ways a more interesting composer – wrote *Abinu malkenu* for violin and orchestra based on a penitential Ashkenazic melody in the early 1970s. More recently, Chris Dench has delved into aspects of Jewish mysticism in works like *'atsiluth*, but it is his student Adam Yee (born 1974) who has consistently drawn on Jewish imagery for his small but distinguished output of work. Yee's first acknowledged work dates from 1994. *Shiru l'adonai shir Hadash*, like much of Yee's subsequent work, takes its title from the Psalms, in this case Psalm 96 'Sing the Lord a new song! Sing to the Lord all the earth!' It is a very assured piece of complex late-modernist writing for clarinet, violin, flute and amplified guitar, characterised by long chords which explode into intricate, polyphonic patterns. Yee makes use of rapid and extreme changes of dynamics, microtonal intervals and extended instrumental techniques. The rhythmic and metrical density insures an ecstatically kaleidoscopic texture; a new song indeed. A much more recent work, *Hallelu et Hasheim min hashamayim* (2007) takes its title from Psalm 148, which calls on the whole of creation, heaven and earth, mountains and hills, fire, ice and snow, to praise the Lord. Rather than producing a Mahlerian symphony, Yee's work is a 20-minute tour-de-force for solo flute, again using a variety of tone productions, non-diatonic intervals and extreme dynamics. As flautist Elizabeth Barcan put it, 'the attempt to represent the rejoicing of the entire universe on a mere flute was certainly a big ask.'[2] But it works. Yee's method lately has involved the use of software programs to elaborate musical information in much less time than a human brain would take. He can generate limitless variations on rhythmic and thematic patterns, and *Hallelu et Hasheim min hashamayim* sought to prove that, working in the single dimension of melody. As we noted in the discussion of Michael Smetanin's work, the 'algorithmic' method is not necessarily restrictive of creative choice. And the poetry in numbers that Yee discovers has a long history as a proof of divine agency.

While not overtly religious, much of the work of Constantine Koukias (born 1965) builds on his Australian Greek Orthodox heritage; in the opera *Days and Nights with Christ*, images of hellish suffering, purification and salvation powerfully dramatise the experience of mental illness. Religious mysticism has been a driving force behind the music of Georges Lentz: the *"Caeli enarrant …"* works take their title from a Latin (Vulgate) version of Psalm 19, and the use of *Mysterium* as a title is a giveaway. Recent works of Ross Edwards, notably his symphonies, have likewise explored western mysticism in conjunction with Edwards' own 'Australian' vernacular.

Constantine Koukias: At the Sound of the Bell

There are, or were, some survivors along the foreshore of Sydney Harbour. Huge enclosed wharves like timber cathedrals built over the water; some, like the Sydney Theatre Company's Wharf theatre have been converted for post-industrial use, but it was in the bare interior of an unrenovated one that the Sydney Festival presented *Days and Nights with Christ*, composed by Constantine Koukias, artistic director of the Hobart-based IHOS Music Theatre and Opera. The work had premiered in 1990, but featured in the Sydney Festival two years later. The Festival's marketing people felt moved to include the rider 'not a religious work' on their advertising. This was probably wise, as it was neither Mel Gibson's *Passion of the Christ* nor World Youth Day; it did, however, offer a powerful experience of the hellish suffering of a young schizophrenic who did in the end reach a state of comfort.

Koukias' theatrical conceptions are as much spatial and visual as musical. For *Days and Nights with Christ*, the audience entered the vast space of the darkened wharf and sat on bleachers facing each other across a central playing space strewn with leaves. At the far end of the playing area was a mountain of salt and a giant block of ice. A mixed ensemble of woodwind, brass and electro-acoustic instruments was placed close to the audience. The ensemble plays music sometimes reminiscent of ecclesiastical chant, but often frenzied and chaotic, howling and jeering. The central character, 'the Man' – played by a dancer – staggers and writhes, crashes into hanging gas cylinders that chime furiously, strips himself naked, screams and weeps, falls to crawling and searches through the withered leaves. His long-suffering

Christos Linou in Constantine Koukias' *Days and Nights with Christ*. Photo by Shirley Apthorp.

mother (played by an actor speaking modern Greek) bears his abuse, bathes and clothes him, and tries, unsuccessfully, to prevent him from harming himself.

There is no 'plot' as conventionally defined – rather the atemporal, hallucinatory states of mind which those of us who haven't experienced it must imagine to constitute this kind of illness. In contrast to the chaotic music and long periods of charged silence, there are two still points: a figure listed as St George, leaf-clad and singing both countertenor and baritone, emerges from the salt mountain and blesses the Man – now handcuffed to prevent self-mutilation and as a metaphor for his condition – with water while singing 'You are the salt of the earth' in ecclesiastical Greek. And in the work's final *coup de théâtre* the great doors of the wharf open to reveal an angel (sung by a soprano drawing a huge white parachute behind her) whose aria – an ecstatic version of St George's music – urges the Man not to fear life and unlocks the handcuffs. He crawls painfully towards a curtain of water under which he stands, cruciform, before collapsing in tears. His mother reclothes him, and together they walk towards the light. Not a religious work? Well, not conventionally, but one which uses powerful imagery and stagecraft to depict the private hell of mental illness and offer the promise of healing if not redemption from it. An opera? Yes. The musical structure is not elaborate, nor was meant to be, but out of the braying trombone, the electro-acoustic atmospherics, the simple chants, the keening, Koukias has created a compelling portrait of a soul in agony and has done so in sounds, in music.

Days and Nights with Christ was the first of Koukias' projects with IHOS. Subsequent works include *To Traverse Water*, based on the experiences of his immigrant Greek mother, a show which blends various musical traditions, such as folk and opera, and other media including film, dance and installations. *TESLA – Lightning in his Hand* about the pioneer of electricity and wireless transmission, Nikola Tesla, and *Olegas*, based on the life of Lithuanian-born Tasmanian photographer Olegas Truchanas, both explore the lives of individuals concerned with elemental forces. Two other works are more frankly concerned with the numinous; *The Divine Kiss* explores the imagery of the seven cardinal virtues while *Prayer Bells – PENTEKOSTARION* is a distillation of liturgical chants from three traditions, the Greek, Roman and Hebrew. Koukias also invokes Gnosticism, a movement which believed in the creation of the world by a demiurge (a kind of divine architect not to be confused with the unknowable Supreme Being). *Prayer Bells* is the least theatrical of Koukias' work, though of course liturgy is essentially dramatic; it is also perhaps the 'purest' musically, in that it doesn't bring together as diverse musical styles as the other works. It is also the 'purest' in the resources required: three cantors (one for each tradition), an eight-voice male choir, percussive sounds made by stones and treated with digital delay, and sixty-one bells in six sets of eleven tuned in quarter-tones between A and D.

The bells were cast especially by Anton Hasell and Neil McLachlan of Australian Bell.[3] The company cast the Federation Bells, installed at Melbourne's Birrarung Marr, and the sets of Federation Hand Bells which can be hired from the Museum of Victoria. They are extraordinary instruments, an attempt to bring together the traditions of European and Asian temple bells. They are open mouthed and are struck (or bowed, or dipped in water while ringing to bend their pitch in the case of Koukias' piece) rather than having an internal clapper. They produce an extraordinarily pure sound, and in *Prayer Bells* create a luminous haze around the deep resonance of the male voices.

The texts are drawn from several sources. The Hebrew chants are largely from Genesis, specifically detailing the creation and God's decision to bring the Flood on evil humanity. The Greek texts are from the Gospels (John's account of the resurrection) and various liturgical forms, and the Latin from devotional poetry by medieval mystic poets Sedulius Scottus, who hymns the risen Christ in the physical world, and Paulinus of Nola who describes the resurrection in imagery of daybreak. This serene and hypnotic music closes with affirmations of light and life from all three cantors.

Christopher Willcock: Marginal Notes

In the early 1960s the second Vatican council revolutionised the liturgy of the Catholic Church: Latin was replaced as the liturgical language by the local vernacular, and clergy were encouraged to make local musical traditions, particularly outside Europe, part of the daily life of the church. Composers were called on to 'produce compositions which have the qualities proper to genuine sacred music, not confining themselves to works which can be sung only by large choirs, but providing also for the needs of small choirs and for the active participation of the entire assembly of the faithful'.[4] That 'active participation' included congregational singing of parts of the Ordinary of the Mass – Lord have mercy, Glory to God in the highest and so on – and the repeated antiphon of the Responsorial Psalm (the verse which is used as a refrain) as well as hymns. In order to entice hitherto silent congregations into singing, many composers cultivated popular idioms – hence the caricature figure of the guitar-toting nun.

Christopher Willcock emerged as a composer of new liturgical music in the 1970s. He studied piano with Alexander Sverjensky at the Sydney Conservatorium of Music, and composition with Peter Sculthorpe at the University of Sydney. He was ordained a Jesuit priest in 1977, having joined the order in 1969, and undertook doctoral studies in Paris. He is currently on the staff of the United Faculty of Theology at the University of Melbourne.

Willcock's large body of liturgical music is perfectly suited to its purpose while never slipping into the ease of cliché. His setting of Psalm 139 offers a good example. For the antiphon, which is sung first by the cantor and then repeated as a refrain by the congregation, Willcock writes a simple but extremely beautiful tune. The antiphon's text, 'How rich are the depths of God', is from Paul's letter to the Romans (11:33); the melody's gentle downwards drift towards those depths is enlivened by an octave leap at 'his wisdom', and the air of mystery and possibility is enhanced by the simple use of an unexpected chord at the end of the phrase.

Willcock's artistic judgment means his liturgical music is at once beautiful and perfectly within the competence of a parish choir and congregation. Since the late 1990s, however, Willcock has begun to produce works for the concert hall, and in doing so has been able to stretch his compositional wings in writing for professional performers. Much of his concert work to date has, unsurprisingly, had some vocal component, and the texts to which he is drawn frequently have some spiritual or urgent moral purpose. In 1998 we saw the premiere of *Five Days Old*, a setting of poetry by Francis Webb for chorus and orchestra, and in 2001 Willcock completed his *Akhmatova Requiem*, setting versions by DM Thomas of the great Russian's searing indictment of the Stalinist terror.

In 2000, Willcock was commissioned by Musica Viva Australia to compose a short work for the Tallis Scholars' national tour. Willcock chose a poem by fellow Jesuit Andrew Bullen, explaining in his own program note that:

> taking its inspiration from the illuminations found in mediaeval manuscripts, Andrew Bullen's poem 'Gospel Bestiary' is a not-too-serious evocation of the images of animals that populate the pages of what are often quite serious theological or philosophical treatises. The poem arranges these animals, all mentioned in the Gospels, into two groups: an 'A-team' constituted by the four living creatures that represent the four evangelists, and a 'B-team' that contains the rest of the menagerie, from the unfortunate Gadarene swine to the donkey that was enlisted for Jesus' entry into Jerusalem. I have therefore given the animals in the A-team a more solemn, ritualized music, whilst the animals in the B-team are treated more variously, with music that employs dance rhythms and word-painting. The setting is written for voices in five parts a cappella, with frequent subdivisions within each part.[5]

Willcock's piece begins with an arresting gesture. The word 'ah!' is in a recognisable but inflected C major. A Lombard rhythm (or Scotch snap) gives it the effect of bouncing off a short consonant chord on the downbeat to a more dissonant longer one. The harmony establishes its rich chromaticism early on, and we also hear a Phrygian motif (a rising and falling semitone flowed by a falling minor third) which will pervade the piece. The tessitura in these 'A-team' sections is very wide, spanning the low C of the second bass to the soprano's top A, and the bass parts often gain rich resonance from lying a fifth apart; it becomes even wider after the leaping major ninth that announces 'the lion of Mark' and when it 'breaks the confines of its uncial[6] *cage'* the sudden appearance of D sharp minor is dramatic.

The 'B-team' section which follows is characterised by short, repeated bird-like motifs for the fowls of the air and fishes; the Gadarene swine tumble down the margin (as they tumble into the sea of Galilee in Mark's Gospel account) in a sequence based on the Phrygian motif in octaves between tenor and bass.

The A-team, now represented by the ox of Luke, alternates A minor and C minor (a relationship which has connotations of mystery in much contemporary film music), but the Phrygian motif emerges when it 'stamps its foot'.

Now the B-team again: scorpions and snakes lurk in the bass register, represented by short motifs under longer lines for alto and tenor. Crowds, well fed by the miracle of loaves and fishes, 'do basketfuls of sums' − a line provokes the composer to indulge in a little 'sight gag' of his own: the metre is '$\frac{3}{16} + \frac{3}{8}$', and so on, before the music trails off into the attenuation 'of crumbs'.

The man who symbolises Matthew is embodied in a simply homophonic version of the A-team music, providing a neat contrast to the B-team's foxes' holes that are represented by semiquaver rests in jaunty rhythm. Jonah and the whale are heard, under the sea, in the tenor and bass register. The people's clamour and donkey bearing Jesus into Jerusalem on Palm Sunday cause a rising in the tessitura to almost purely diatonic cries of 'hosanna'.

The eagle of John relates to the lion of Mark with the rising ninth as he 'stares into the sun', which in turn floods the music with a new tonality based on a B flat major ninth chord. A reprise of the Phrygian motif leads to the last section 'All beasts ...' which reconciles A and B teams. Sheep and goats are separated, naturally, judged by the 'gold initials of the Lord'. These are imaged by a lovely luminous homophony, ushering in a vision of the peaceable kingdom. A final 'Ah!' takes the music to its closing D major.

Mary Finsterer and the Metaphoric Gateway

Contemporary art music doesn't generally have a reputation for being thigh-slappingly funny, and it's fair to say that many composers describe their work in terms which can be serious to the point of dourness.

There is also a residual idea that dissonance, as traditionally understood, necessarily expresses 'negative' feelings: pain, anger, madness.
To be fair, many composers in post-war Europe had sound political
and artistic reasons for exploring
those emotions. But the arrival of
Hungarian composer György Ligeti
among the ranks of the European
avant-garde in the 1950s put paid to

some of those ideas when it became obvious that the composer had a
comic streak as well as musical genius, and an ability to work in the
most 'advanced' idioms.

Mary Finsterer has cultivated an advanced musical idiom since the
late 1980s. Her work is characterised by intricate surfaces created in
part by extended instrumental techniques and complex pitch organisation, but this hasn't precluded her, on occasions, from writing pieces
which can only be described as fun. In 1992 the ABC commissioned
Finsterer to compose a fanfare for the Melbourne Symphony Orchestra to play at the opening of the Next Wave youth arts festival. The
Next Wave Fanfare is a big, loud, energetically anarchic piece in which
Finsterer:

> wanted to create for the audience the sense of being a child again –
> of going to the fair for the first time and seeing big whirling colourful
> objects like Ferris wheels and big dippers – and being thrilled if not a
> little scared by these monstrous and strange mechanical animals.[7]

Similarly, the trio *Catch*, for soprano saxophone, bass clarinet and
piano, begins with a punning title which refers both to a children's
game and to a musical form popular in Tudor and Jacobean England.
There is no lack of rigour or complexity in the writing, but the effect
of the piece is joyous.

Finsterer studied at the University of Melbourne with, among
others, Brenton Broadstock and in 1993 spent a year in Amsterdam
studying with Louis Andriessen. But in many respects her musical
personality was already fully formed, as one can hear in the cham-

ber orchestral *Ruisselant* of 1991 – arguably her 'breakthrough' piece. This work was commissioned by Le Nouvel Ensemble Moderne based in Montreal and premiered by it. A glance at the score is illuminating: there are fully eleven pages of performance notes at the start, meticulously detailing how various unconventional sounds should be produced, the precise fingerings of string harmonics and wind multiphonics, and the notation of ornamental figures such as mordents. The title, literally 'Streaming', is both poetic and technically descriptive. As Finsterer notes, *ruisselant* is a word which appears abundantly in French literature, and here it refers to the image of flowing water, the sense of time unfolding through music and the structural process of this particular piece. The process of 'streaming' works on a number of levels, note to note, motif to motif and section to section, and, as Finsterer puts it, 'the direct opposition or synchronisation of streams … is the very essence pervading the human condition'.[8] We get some sense of what this might mean from the work's opening, where very short, loud chords from woodwinds, brass and the lowest reaches of piano and double bass release staggered eddies of glittering harmonics from the second violin, viola and cello. The streams of harmonics become longer and interlock; this fluttering delicacy is echoed in the many passages where mordents give the instrumental lines a quivering vibrancy, as rhythmic fragments high in the piano and piccolo begin to coalesce into fragments of melody. A contrasting second section is less pointillistic, with emphatic, repeated figures emerging from the brass that gradually encompass the entire orchestra. The final section begins again with more aerated textures – short gestures bounce around the orchestra before more relentless tutti scoring takes up most of the work's concluding section.

Finsterer's remark about the 'essence of the human condition' suggests that for her, music is about more than music, though as she freely admits, often her titles come to her during or after the process of composition. These are often intriguing and refer to a wide range of interests: the 'concerto grosso' *Nyx*, for instance, refers to the mythological Greek goddess of night. An example of the composer's abiding interest in ancient cultures, the piece is, like *Catch*, nonetheless essentially comic.

By 'comic' I don't simply mean fun. Dante's *Commedia* isn't a laugh a minute, but is idealistic about humanity's prospects; Shakespeare's comedies are funny, but more importantly end with the imagery of reconciliation and resolution. This is not unrelated to some of the 'spiritual' concerns in Finsterer's work. Her short work for cello and orchestra, *Ascension and Descend* was inspired by a series of photographs of stairs by Dean Golja, which he in turn describes as a 'metaphoric gateway that could have the power to transport the imagination to another dimension, whether it be aesthetic or spiritual'.[9]

The most specifically 'spiritual' work in Finsterer's output is her *Omaggio alla Pietà* for six voices and percussion (there is an optional double bass part in the score). The work grew out of a project instigated by Sydney conductor Roland Peelman for his estimable vocal group, the Song Company in 1993. The project *Via crucis Australis : an Australian journey of the Cross* was based on the Stations (or Way) of the Cross, a Catholic liturgy these days celebrated on the morning of Good Friday, in which the congregation enacts the journey of Christ to Golgotha. The fourteen stations begin with the death-sentence and conclude with the entombment. Peelman commissioned a different composer for each station, each of which was represented by a newly commissioned work of visual art; the performance took place in the Museum of Contemporary Art in Sydney.

Finsterer's work depicts the thirteenth station, the Deposition, where Jesus' body is taken down from the Cross. The gospel accounts agree that Joseph of Arimathea received permission from Pontius Pilate to bury the body. St John's includes another supporter, Nicodemus; the three other gospels suggest that Mary Magdalene and Jesus' mother were among 'many women from Jerusalem' who witnessed the crucifixion and followed Joseph to the tomb. Much Catholic iconography conflates this into an image of the crucified Christ laid in his mother's arms: its most famous expression is in Michelangelo's *Pietà*.

For her text Finsterer uses a set of poems by Jacinta Le Plastrier, *Songs*

The Song Company rehearsing Mary Finsterer's *Omaggio alla Pietà*.
Photo by Dean Golja.

for Mary, verses which powerfully concentrate key images of Jesus' life,
(for instance, recalling her son's life as a carpenter, Mary sings of 'this
hand/ shaped as mine/ drove wood into song ...') as well as expressing
Mary's horror, grief and ultimate prayer for the forgiveness of Jesus'
killers. The work's form is reminiscent of the three-voiced motet cultivated in late medieval Europe. In those works of the Ars Nova, the
tenor states a plainchant melody in slow motion over which the *motetus*
and *triplum* weave independent melodies, often using independent but
simultaneously sounded texts. In *Omaggio alla Pietà* the contralto takes
the role of *tenor* (though not, of course, using a plainchant) in that she
sings the most consistent and elaborated line to three of Le Plastrier's

poems. This is a woman at breaking point. Her extremely low tessitura (the line clings doggedly to the F sharp below the treble stave, occasionally jumping to a distant interval before returning) and sobbing melismas remind us that this is the *mater dolorosa*. High above the contralto, the two sopranos give a more fragmentary account of the remaining text. Their lines are much more disjunct, and are heterophonic – that is, more or less in unison but with decorations and deviations which create moments of sudden instability. The male voices produce a third element, declaiming fragments of the Easter sequence, or hymn, *Victimae paschali laudes immolent Christiani* (Christians, praise the Paschal victim who was sacrificed). The texts, like thematic material in other works of Finsterer's, gradually move to new voices: all but the contralto urgently sing the Latin fragment in the last pages of the piece, as the contralto sings 'have mercy on them'. All singers use extended techniques – whispering, clapping, exaggerating the production of consonants. The percussion part occasionally permits itself the comfort of bells, but more typically offers a febrile scattering of wood and skin. This is deeply disturbing music, as well it might be.

Nigel Butterley and the Spell of Creation

Unlike direct contemporaries like Peter Sculthorpe and Richard Meale, Nigel Butterley did not find a distinctive voice in reflecting on landscape, or overt engagement with either doctrinaire modernism or non-European music. The tradition he embodies, and has adapted to local conditions, is a particularly British one: like Ralph Vaughan Williams, Benjamin Britten and Michael Tippett, Butterley expresses an undogmatic spirituality which is profoundly humanitarian; like theirs his music is extremely personal and idiosyncratic in style. In major works from the 1960s to the present, Butterley explores the numinous – a sense that the divine can be experienced, if only briefly, in and through the physical universe. For Butterley music is about the communication of extra-musical ideas. His output therefore includes a high proportion of vocal music and he is especially drawn to ecstatic religious poetry from a variety of cultures. Various works employ sacred texts from ancient Middle Eastern and Indian religions and medieval Christian mystics; he has also explored that loose grouping of seventeenth century 'Metaphysical' poets like John Donne, Henry Vaughan and Thomas Traherne who used virtuosic, post-Shakespearean language to explore complex religious experience. On occasion too Butterley has used ciphers – musical motifs which symbolise, or even spell out, specific words or concepts. His highly personal musical language grows out of the impulse to communicate precise, though not necessarily verbal, meaning. This is most striking in a harmony that is characterised by a pervasive dissonance which can range from imperceptibly mild to strikingly astringent; the 'vision splendid' doesn't come easy.

The work which signals the beginning of his maturity as a composer, *Laudes*, for mixed instrumental octet, was composed in 1963 at the invitation of Professor Donald Peart for the Adelaide Festival; in 1967 it represented Australia at the Paris Rostrum. At the time of composition, Butterley had just returned from a year's study in London with Priaulx Rainier, and had gathered strong impressions of features of four European churches. The Basilica of Sant'Apollinaire Nuovo in Ravenna, the Apse of Norwich Cathedral, King's College Chapel at Cambridge and The Church of Reconciliation at the Community of Taizé in Burgundy each form the basis of a movement of the work.

In 1966 the ABC gave Butterley his first formal commission, asking for a radiophonic work to be entered in the prestigious Italia Prize. *In the Head the Fire*, a 'musical collage' for radio, won ahead of Luciano Berio's *Laborintus II*. With technology which these days seems practically steam-driven – essentially a collage of tape recordings – Butterley produced a work of enormous power. This piece explores various ideas of mysticism, and to that end the composer assembled texts from sources as diverse as the Dead Sea Scrolls, ancient Irish mystical poetry (from which the title is taken), the Mass, and passages in Hebrew, Latin and Greek. The texts are sung and spoken; the instrumental parts include orchestral woodwind and brass, recorders, piano, organ, percussion and *shofar*, the ram's-horn trumpet associated with Jewish ritual. Through manipulation of some hundred individual recordings, the component parts are layered and woven into a dramatic arch form of a half-hour's duration. The work is, in a word, *composed* by the architectural structuring of its disparate events in time.

The orchestral *Meditations of Thomas Traherne* of 1968 reflects his interest in English metaphysical writing. *Traherne* is classic Butterley: each of its five linked movements fans out from, and returns to, a single note, as it were miming the process of meditation on a single idea. Traherne's meditations are on the nature of eternity, 'a Mysterious Absence of Times and Ages ... Ev'ry Man is alone the Centre and Circumference of it.'[10] Traherne laments that 'The World is a Mirror of infinit Beauty, yet no Man sees it' and like the later poet Wordsworth notes that only the eyes of childhood truly see the 'innumerable joys' of the universe. Butterley's musical image of the child, or 'little stranger', is brilliant in its simplicity: a recorder consort touchingly conjures the world of childhood set in high relief against the sophisticated sound of the orchestra.

Butterley is also drawn to poets like Emily Dickinson and Walt Whitman. His *Sometimes with one I love*, for speaker, soprano, baritone and mixed ensemble, sets poetry and prose of Whitman, as does another radiophonic work, *Watershore*, but the influence is equally to be felt in a number of purely instrumental pieces. The String Quartet No. 2 is headed by lines from *Leaves of Grass*, and the solo piano piece, *Uttering Joyous Leaves* (written as a test piece for the Sydney International Piano Competition), takes its title from a Whitman poem about the need for love and companionship.

Butterley was a practising Anglican until 1969, but his withdrawal from organised religion allowed him to develop a syncretic spirituality, bringing together complementary strands from a variety of different cultural sources. Moreover, much of his work throughout the 1970s and 1980s specifically explores transcendence, the notion of reality beyond the immediately apprehended physical world. This is behind even a fairly abstract work like *Explorations* for piano and orchestra written for the celebrations of the Captain Cook Bicentenary in 1970, where the notion of exploring becomes part of the process of composition.

Transcendence is also a major concern behind Butterley's 1988 opera *Lawrence Hargrave Flying Alone*. Hargrave, also the subject of Barry Conyngham's opera *Fly*, was an Australian inventor, explorer and scientist whose designs for heavier-than-air flying machines were crucial though unacknowledged steps in the development of aviation. Butterley first became interested in Hargrave when he saw a sculpture by Tasmanian artist Peter Taylor depicting Hargrave passing, spirit-like, through a solid wooden door (the piece is now in the composer's collection). Butterley and his librettist James McDonald developed the metaphor of Hargrave's transcendental vision into a kind of 'miracle play' – a series of self-contained scenes, each of which demonstrates an aspect of Hargrave's character: as a hero in a shipwreck, as a brilliant inventor, as an explorer who sees the destructive potential of exploration. The work's two acts are symmetrical in construction, an image of the wings that inspired Hargrave's research into aeronautics. It is of course tempting to see Hargrave the visionary as a kind of cipher for Butterley the composer, particularly in the single-minded way in which each has been prepared to follow a very personal vision, alone.

For some years now Butterley has had a strong interest in the poetry and critical writings of British poet Kathleen Raine. Raine is of the Auden, Spender and MacNeice generation; unlike them she continued a tradition of metaphysical thought, in her poetry and writings on such figures as William Blake. A number of Butterley's works from the 1990s on, such as the symphonic *From Sorrowing Earth* (1991), are directly inspired by Raine's writings and ideas. The orchestral song cycle *The Woven Light* (1994) crystallises Butterley's recurrent themes of loss and transcendent reality. The woven light of the title is Raine's symbol for the ideal or eternal world shrouded by physical existence. In the poems set by Butterley it is glimpsed 'once', and while 'to have seen/Is to know always', the song cycle's conclusion is not unambiguously affirmative. Butterley's music deals with its own imagery of the hidden, of the bleak landscapes which Raine evokes in 'I came too late to the hills'. His orchestration tends on such occasions to be dense, making for a breathtaking contrast at those moments where the transcendental is glimpsed, such as at the climax of the third song.

Spell of Creation

Spell of Creation, scored for soprano and baritone soloists, semi-chorus, double chorus and large orchestra, is a summation of those musical and metaphysical ideas which have run through Butterley's work since the early 1960s: it is in part a hymn to the physical universe, and the connotations of both enchantment and writing are implicit in the word 'spell'. It uses a wide range of sacred and spiritual texts, drawn in this case from *The Book of Ba'al* (a religious text from Ugarit, a city on what is now the Syrian coast which flourished around 1450–1200 BC); verses by medieval Christian mystics Hildegard of Bingen and Julian of Norwich; the Vedic *Taittīrya Brāhmana* (written in Sanskrit some centuries BC); and poems by Henry Vaughan and Kathleen Raine. Like *The Woven Light* it is heavily informed by Kathleen Raine's vision of the ideal partly occluded from view. Elliott Gyger's program note for the work's premiere quotes Butterley's statement that *Spell of Creation* 'contrasts the perceived ("God" who can be praised) with the unknowable (The Divine Ineffable). Attempts to apprehend and to praise become more and more frantic, as they can never fully succeed. The Unknowable prevails.'[11]

Like *Lawrence Hargrave Flying Alone*, the design of *Spell of Creation* is dominated by symmetries. Of its five movements, the odd-numbered ones tend to be the most complex and extrovert, using composite texts; the second and fourth are more introspective and concentrate on Raine's poetry.

The work begins with a mysterious texture. Very softly, tuned gongs and harp outline a series of narrow intervals (around middle C) which are slowly decorated by a trio of flutes (one of them an alto) at the lowest extreme of their range. Male voices and muted horns enter, the singers intoning verses from the *Book of Ba'al*: 'Offer bread to the earth/ Plant in the ground the tree of love …'. Middle Eastern cultures such as

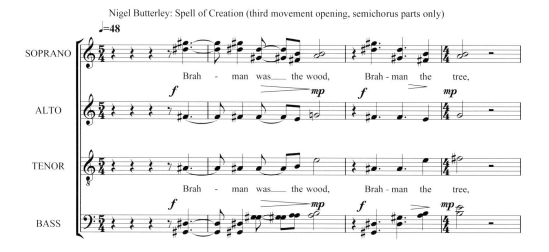

Nigel Butterley: Spell of Creation (third movement opening, semichorus parts only)

Nigel Butterley: *Spell of Creation* third movement opening, semi-chorus part only. Notice the ecstatic use of mild dissonance and high-lying vocal writing. Used by permission of the composer.

Ugarit worshipped a pantheon whose supreme god was El, but who had delegated the rule of the earth to his son Ba'al. (A fierce local tribe of monotheistic nomads, the Hebrews, took great exception to this. Ba'al is referred to in the Hebrew Bible as a false god, as in the incident where Elijah wins a contest with Ba'al's priests, and his title Prince Ba'al, or Beelzebub, soon became an epithet for the Devil.) Graham Williams, a Sydney journalist, introduced Butterley to the *Book of Ba'al*, who made a version of several lines in which there is nothing but cosmic harmony, 'the light of love upon the fields ...'. The music becomes more urgent, with rising motifs gathering speed and volume as they pass from low brass through woodwinds and strings until the chorus's 'Hasten, for I have a word to tell you', a secret offering of revelation. Butterley's deployment of the vocal lines is arresting, with entries from the full choir, semi-chorus and soloists staggered, each softer, to suggest echoes in a vast space supported by a soft hum of low strings. Material from the opening provides a bridge into the movement's central section, a setting of the medieval mystic Hildegard of Bingen's hymn *O nobilissima viriditas*. *Viriditas*, with its connotations of both 'strength' and 'greenness' (a word which she possibly coined), has a resonance in the text set by Butterley with 'planting the tree of love'.

Butterley sets *O nobilissima viriditas* for double choir accompanied largely by antiphonal bursts of brass sound. The harmony has a certain radiance in its preference for open intervals, inflected by the relatively consonant clash of major seconds (the first chord for instance is, from the bottom up, C, D, A, D), and the echo effect is enhanced by the second choir's shadowing the first a beat or so later. A climax on the words *ut solis flamma* (the sun's blaze) returns us to the *Book of Ba'al*'s promise of revelation: 'word of the tree and whisper of the stone'. The movement concludes with lines by Kathleen Raine, sung by the soprano and baritone soloists and accompanied by a spare texture of quiet brass and woodwind and muted strings.

The second movement begins with angular two-part counterpoint for violins, recalling some of Michael Tippett's work, answered by a wash of mainly stepwise, upward-moving figures for woodwinds. The baritone sings lines from Raine's poem *Shells* about reaching down into the sea to gather shells, and reaches an ecstatic climax at the image of 'forms … shaped on the day of creation'. The shells 'whisper for ever in our ears'; this brings in the semi-chorus in a chordal passage spread right across the vocal range from the bass's low F to the soprano's top A flat: softly they sing 'The world that you inhabit has not yet been created'. This precipitates a faster, vertiginous coda characterised by frequent changes of time signature and uneven rhythmic groupings. 'Into what pattern into music have the spheres whirled us?' sings the full (double) choir, now in a maximum of four parts. But the vision fades at the word 'transfigurations', the high strings, flutes, stopped horns and glockenspiel coming to rest on a glowing chord (the first five notes of the B flat major scale spread out over an octave and a half).

Deep knotted dissonances from bass clarinet, contrabassoon, low strings, trombones, percussion and harp contrast strikingly with the choir's first entry in the third movement. Ba'al's tree of love, and Hildegard's *viriditas* 'whose roots are in sunlight' morph into the semi-chorus' joyous cry — a harmony full of open, perfect intervals over a huge span (related to the harmony at 'The world that you inhabit has not yet been created') — 'Brahman was the wood, Brahman was the tree from which they shaped heaven and earth.' The words 'heaven' and 'earth' release ornate melismatic writing (that is, more than one note — in this case many notes — per syllable).

'Brahman was the wood' comes from the *Taittīrya Brāhmana*, a subsection of the *Yajur Veda*, which Butterley came across in *An Illustrated Encyclopaedia of Traditional Symbols* by JC Cooper. He was researching a new piece for cellist David Pereira, who had recently acquired a new instrument built from Australian timber; it was also at this time that a Huon pine, discovered in Tasmania, was thought to be the world's oldest living organism. One of the four most ancient Indian scriptures, the *Yajur Veda* probably existed in oral form as far back as 1200 BC, but was written in Sanskrit in about 600 BC. The Vedas provide a repository of much of the mythology and liturgy of the subcontinent, with hymns to various deities and details of the rituals and sacrifices appropriate to them. The god Brahman, in this cosmology, is not so much the Supreme Being as the Ground of Being; all things, including the bewildering pantheon of gods and goddesses are, despite their variety and difference, all manifestations of Brahman.

In various iconographies and texts Brahman is depicted in the image of the tree, often, as in the later *Katha Upanishad*, with its 'roots aloft [that is, in heaven] and its branches spread below [on earth]'. In Hindu theology, the idea that we are separate from Brahman is an illusion; from here it is a short step to the next text that Butterley sets: an excerpt from Raine's 'Message from home'. Raine, like Wordsworth in his Ode, *Intimations of Immortality from Recollections of Early Childhood*, tries to recapture the 'vision splendid', the sense of harmony with the universe, experienced by the unselfconscious child.

In a lightly inflected C major the soloists sing an ecstatic duet to Raine's question 'Do you remember, when you were first a child/ nothing in the world seemed strange to you? ... before you became estranged from your own being ...'. The scoring is very light, seldom in more than two parts (and derived from the violin counterpoint at the beginning of the second movement). The image of the 'sun's rays' conjures a reminiscence of the opening 'Offer bread to the earth' chorus, now for a trio of cellos. This introduces the choir's soft, spacious chords which support the soloists' 'Sleep at the tree's root, where night is spun into the stuff of worlds ...' before a return to the 'Brahman was the wood ...' cry from the semi-chorus. This in turn leads to the second of Hildegard's hymns, *Spiritus sanctus vivificans vita* (Holy Spirit, you are life itself and life-giving), a vibrant setting once again for double chorus which makes use of antiphonal effects provided by a slight delay between each group's entries. The movement ends contemplatively, with a restatement of the *Book of Ba'al*'s 'Offer bread to the earth'.

The fourth movement is structurally the simplest in the work. A short orchestral introduction again recalls 'Offer bread to the earth', and makes use of characteristic textures like the widely spaced string chords and gently shimmering woodwind triplets. Then the choir, divided antiphonally, sings the 'title track', Raine's *Spell of Creation*. This poem could trace its lineage through such lyrics as the 'Corpus Christi Carol' to the riddles, spells and gnomic verses of Anglo-Saxon poetry. Like Russian stacking dolls, each image acts as a frame for the one which follows: 'within the flower there lies a seed, in the seed there springs a tree, in the tree there spreads a wood ...' and so on, seamlessly threading the natural world together with that of the spirit and love. The moment of transformation comes when 'in the bird there beats a heart, and from the heart flows a song', at which point the vocal lines become floridly melismatic, leading to the 'word [where] speaks a world'.

Raine's unification of the universe through imagery and syntax prepares us for the final summing up of Butterley's vision in the fifth and final movement. The full chorus revisits the Book of Ba'al's 'word of the tree' to be answered by the semi-chorus's ecstatic 'Brahman was the wood'; a short passage alternating between the two brings these strikingly similar images from wildly different traditions into unity.

From this now familiar material the music gathers a new urgency, as the soloists sing the opening lines 'I saw Eternity the other night' from the 'metaphysical' poet Henry Vaughan's *The World*.

Despite the image of eternity as 'calm as it was bright', there is an urgency to Butterley's setting of the opening lines, as if the music is aware of how quickly the vision splendid can and will fade. The vocal lines are highly melismatic, especially stressing words like 'light' and Butterley repeats words and phrases ('I saw', 'eternity') against an orchestral texture where broad throbbing triplets for trumpets or flutes are overlaid with faster, febrile semiquavers and sextuplets. These begin in the lower woodwinds and strings but gradually work their way up through the orchestral mass. By the end of this musical paragraph, the image of the world hurled through space conjures a busy, loud orchestral palette which finally bursts out in a section marked *barbaro*. This is the final setting of Hildegard, a hymn to Wisdom portrayed as a three-winged creature 'encompassing us'. As before, the full chorus is divided into antiphonal halves, but now the harmony is more often simultaneous (rather than the delayed echoing effect of earlier). Buoyed by emphatic rhythmic expostulations from the brass, the section reaches a big climax at the words 'Laus tibi sit' (praise to you). All choral parts are high in their register (the first sopranos, for instance, hover around their top G, reaching B flat on the word '*Sapientia*', wisdom). After this image of wisdom as the animating force of the universe, the music moves back towards silence, with the solo soprano singing a passage from the fifth of the *Revelations of the Divine Love* by fourteenth century mystic, Julian of Norwich.

In Julian's fifth revelation she is shown 'a little thing, small as a hazelnut in the palm of my hand'. Wondering, she is told by the semi-chorus representing the voice of God that 'it is all that is made'. For this moment Butterley again uses the kind of widely spaced harmony we heard in the second movement ('The world that you inhabit has not yet been created') and the third ('Brahman was the wood'): a pair of chords (F minor with an added second, and A minor with added fourth), sung *pianissimo*, span more than three octaves. From here the music dissolves gradually into silence. A very soft texture of brass, violas and gongs supports aleatoric writing in the upper strings, semi-chorus and the second choir. The first choir sings Raine's *The World*. In this tightly constructed lyric, the images of the first stanza – 'It burns in the void/ nothing upholds it/ still it travels' – combine and recombine. It's like slowly revolving a multi-faceted jewel, until the final 'Nothing it travels/ a burning void/ upheld by silence'. With that, a barely audible bass drum roll fades to nothingness. The vision is fugitive; God has hidden himself again.

Georges Lentz and the Vault of Heaven

Georges Lentz is a paradoxical figure for his time and generation. Born in Luxembourg in 1965, but an Australian resident since 1990, Lentz's music is widely performed in Australia, the EU and USA, yet he rarely accepts commissions and prefers to work, often for years at a time, on a small number of pieces. His musical language is highly idiosyncratic yet succeeds in communicating deeply-held convictions about the nature of the universe; his craftsmanship is of the highest level, but it is wholly at the service of the spiritual program which pervades his entire output. A large body of Lentz's music falls into works or groups of works entitled *"Caeli enarrant …"*, a reference to Psalm 19's vision of the cosmos as the embodiment and proof of divine agency:

> The heavens declare the glory of God,
> The vault of heaven proclaims his handiwork;
> Day discourses of it to day,
> night to night hands on the knowledge.

As the composer has noted: '*"Caeli enarrant …"* is a cycle of pieces reflecting my fascination with astronomy as well as my spiritual beliefs'.[12] We sense, then, an underpinning to Lentz's work related to a certain stream of Christian mysticism – that which includes thinkers from Meister Eckhart and Hildegard of Bingen (discussed in relation to Nigel Butterley's *Spell of Creation*) through to Teilhard de Chardin and Thomas Merton. He also uses contemporary texts, as in the *Seven Last Words* for the Australian Chamber Orchestra, where authors Peter Goldsworthy, Thomas Keneally, Michael Leunig, David Malouf, Dorothy Porter and David Williamson contributed meditations on Christ's final utterances.

Of course Christian mysticism made something of a comeback in western art music in the last decades of the twentieth century. The post-war avant-garde had sought freedom from the cultural weight of the past in the hermetic systems of Boulez, the political activism of Hans Werner Henze and Luigi Nono and the exploration of eastern religion by Cage and Stockhausen. A more recent generation including Arvo Pärt and John Tavener have married a radically simple harmonic palette to a program based on traditional Christian texts. Georges Lentz, by contrast, is undogmatic about both his religious orientation (he is frank about his doubts) and undogmatic about his musical modern-ism: he has felt at liberty, especially in the works from the early 1990s, to use a number of radically different stylistic gambits to achieve his expressive purpose. His harmony ranges between strident density and radiant consonance; his rhythmic gestures can be aphoristic to the point of terseness, or generate considerable momentum. Single pitches can have supreme centrality, or the processes of twentieth-century serialism can be brought into play; melodies range from simple modal phrases to fragmented lines distributed note by note among different voices, rather like the medieval practice of 'hocket'. In these early works, Lentz is also interested in aspects of Tibetan music, notably monastic chant and the sound of the *gyaling*, a double reed instrument which is almost always played in pairs, so that slight modifications of pitch (such as note 'bending') and ornamentation (trills) create an immense variety of expression.

Lentz often works on several pieces concurrently and over a long span of time. He began work on *"Caeli enarrant ... III"* in 1990 and *"Caeli enarrant ... IV"* in 1991, completing both works in 2000. The former is for strings (six violins, three violas, three cellos), three percus-sionists and boy soprano and falls into three movements played without a break. A characteristic gesture acts as a gateway into the piece: swift string glissandos crystallise around a single chime, opening out on a bleak landscape of long-held notes, ricocheting pizzicatos and short, nervous motives. The narrow intervals and microtonal inflections of the next movement reflect Lentz's interest in the Tibetan gyaling. By way of complete contrast, a shower of metallic sound leads into the lambent third movement. Here lush textures and simple harmony support a long-breathed vocal melody redolent of Gregorian chant, before a short reminiscence of some of the work's earlier gestures. The whole piece is generated out of a strict serial process, which, the composer has noted:

> gives the music a sense of rotation and symbolizes the idea of the circle and the spiral, a recurrent feature in the universe. Even the 'beautiful' modal chords towards the end of the work are influenced by the tone row. However, the use of this technique is merely a means of expression, never a dogmatic system. The established rigid pattern is therefore often destroyed in the course of the composition, opening the doors wide to intuition, even randomness.

"*Caeli enarrant … IV*" is for string quartet and four suspended cymbals. There is considerable thematic reference between the work's four movements, and it plays continuously; balancing this is the use of dramatically different musical manners and gestures. Single instruments sound a central pitch (F) in turn, creating a simple, regular rhythm. New tones are progressively added; sudden dissonances demand attention. In the last moments of the movement, the music breaks with the regularity of pulse in favour of more extravagant gestures; a background of soft, sustained high sounds contrasts with disembodied percussive gestures and isolated diatonic harmonies lead straight into the second movement. Here we meet a faster tempo beginning with a fanfare of diatonic chords, use of strongly profiled rhythmic cells and dance rhythms as ostinatos; then a contrasting section based on long-held background chords – with pizzicato figurations gathering to a series of densely dissonant chords characterised by intense 'hairpin' dynamics.

Material from the first part of the movement re-emerges before final cadential chords mask the beginning of the third movement. This is characterised at first by microtonal colouring of a central pitch with increasingly prominent cymbals, a reminiscence of the fanfare chords and busy rhythmic, hocketing unisons. Significantly, a version of the slow part of this movement exists as a work for string orchestra entitled *Te Deum laudamus* of which the composer has written: 'Does it make any sense to 'praise God' while the TV is showing me pictures of Iraq, Rwanda, the Balkans, the Middle East ...? My personal answer to these questions is obviously contained in the music.' Indeed, like Beethoven in the *Heiliger Dankgesang* movement of his String Quartet Op. 132, Lentz evokes a hymnal sound, here by the use of viol-like timbres. Dissonant clusters lurk and burst forth but are interrupted by ringing diatonic upper-register chords. A return to the central tone idea acts as a bridge into the final movement characterised by aleatoric sounds, *flautato* writing and the percussive use of instruments. There is one final arresting gesture and the rest is silence.

Discussing *"Caeli enarrant ... III"*, Lentz once pointed out that:

> one of the central features of the work is *silence*, a precondition to any form of contemplation and an analogy to the absence of (visible) matter in huge portions of the universe. In a world dominated by speed, noise, fun and mass culture, we seem to have lost the patience to abandon ourselves to time and silence. Yet silence has a strange and individual quality. Not every silence is the same. It is 'coloured' by its acoustic environment, i.e. the music that precedes it. It is thus not simply absence of sound, but, as it were, 'spiritual music'. Analogously, I believe that the parts of the universe that do not contain any visible matter are still filled with 'spirit', a higher presence beyond time and space.

In 1994 he began work on the seventh and final part of the *"Caeli enarrant ..."* series, *Mysterium*. This has proved to be a quite new and different enterprise for Lentz. It grew out of his growing interest in the Pythagorean formulation of the Music of the Spheres, which, as the composer puts it, 'is audible to God, but inaudible to human ears'. This ideal, or as John Donne described it, 'equal music', doesn't recognise the opposition of sound and silence, and, unlike human music, does not need space and time to exist. Lentz, therefore, wrote this work as a conceptual piece in open form without fixed instrumentation — 'abstract lines and dots, *ideally* meant to be *read* rather than played'. He is quick to add: 'This may sound naïve, even pretentious — it is hard to attempt this kind of project without seeming overly ambitious.' In order, however, to communicate at least *something* of the composer's vision, some kind of performance must happen, so Lentz has used material from *Mysterium* to create works like *Birrung* (an Aboriginal word meaning 'stars') and *Nguurraa* ('Light'), as well as larger orchestral works like *Ngangkar* and *Guyuhmgan*. As the titles suggest, the Pythagorean vision is mediated for Lentz by an exploration of Australian Aboriginal spirituality (as expressed by painters like Kathleen Petyarre and the late Emily Kame Kngwarreye), but not by an appropriation or imitation of Aboriginal music. Aboriginal cosmology, like the Hebrew Psalmist's, understands the physical world as the 'written' record of divine agency; Lentz suggests that 'one possible way to listen to *Mysterium* might be to simply imagine a starlit sky with all its different constellations and concentrations, its darkness and light, the vastness of its silence'.

The *Mysterium* works are, as a whole, quiet throughout. As Lentz says:

> tension results solely from the polarity between sound and silence, tonal and quarter-tone elements, homophonic lines and complex polyphonic material, a regular crotchet beat and graphically notated rhythmic unpredictability, expanded and contracted time. My overall aim was to write music that would be as 'pure' as possible. Hence the severe self-imposed restrictions.

In *Birrung* (1997), for instance, Lentz draws from the string ensemble a varied array of homophonic and polyphonic textures, and harmony which visits the extremes of dissonance and consonance, but all at a soft dynamic level, and without gestures which impose a sense of closure on the music. Similarly, in *Nguurraa* (2000–01), the clarinet's opening melody might have been playing unheard for some time and the soft piano chords at the end by no means seek to sum up a musical argument but rather point to an ongoing discourse.

Mysterium sets out to uncover an image of the ideal world. This ultimate reality, as Lentz sees it, may or may not turn out to be utopian. Unlike more doctrinaire composers, Lentz is increasingly less inclined to enforce an interpretation through the use of dissonance or noise. His music is aware of the ambiguity of silence:

> The words that perhaps best sum up my spiritual attitude these days would be 'and yet ...'. I can't help doubting many of the dogmas that were inculcated into me as a child, *and yet* I still have an unshakable belief in a higher (metaphysical) reality. This reality may or may not turn out to be a utopia. My way of questioning these ideal worlds in my music is not by shattering them through *ff*-outbursts (in my opinion a cliché), but through the use of silence – the most glorious sound, in one way, but also the most terrible, terrifying one. We all know that eternal silence is our common 'final destination'. Hence my music is, to my mind, also and above all about the problem of bearing this silence, about the problem of *loneliness*. My fascination with lonely places (the Australian Outback, for example) is also a metaphor for this (existential) loneliness.

This recent interpretation of silence is noticeably more ambiguous than the earlier statement from 1996. This is music that admits to both Pascal's terror and Messiaen's joy at the infinities of space. But with the image of the Australian Outback as a metaphor for existential loneliness we are back in the world of Sculthorpe's *Irkanda* series.

Conclusion

Among my late mother's effects I found a small textbook entitled *History of Music* by the Reverend Bonavia Hunt. It must have been published in the four last years of the 19th century, as Verdi was still alive, his only possible successor the 'young composer Mascagni'. Brahms, recently dead, gets an approving sentence – one – as do Charles Gounod, Niels Gade and Ebenezer Prout. You see my problem? First, it would have been impossibly messy to try and include, or to discuss in detail, everyone who composes in this country even if their work were of an even standard and quality. Under the circumstances, I felt that the honourable thing was to omit, among others, discussion of my own music.

Moreover, reputations come and go; sometimes the great white hope turns out to be a disappointment; the 'one least likely to' turns around and does. So, I don't think there are any foolish prophecies in this book, and I have deliberately not written about the younger generation, though it includes some highly talented people. And I have avoided talking about the several younger composers now living and working overseas.

What I have tried to do is give you a sense of the range of composers, their styles, media and aesthetic preoccupations that exist in Australian music today, and to introduce you to music I genuinely love. We have seen that there are composers maintaining the principles of the European avant-garde and composers engaging with various aspects of Asian culture. There are composers working to have new music a normal part of mainstream concert life and others who pursue a deeply personal and sometimes esoteric vision. Whether the detente I mentioned at the beginning of this book is the result of simple apathy or a genuine tolerance of difference is a moot point. I'd like to think it was the latter, and am very grateful that the bile and spite that people spat at each other back in the early 1990s has largely disappeared. It is at best counterproductive, sending a message to the general public – who have been at times very generous in funding many of our activities – that our profession is merely riven with feuds and petty jealousies. Moreover, I like to think that success breeds success, that the more of our music that is heard by the general public the better, as it will engender in that public a further expectation of new work. But for that, the work has to be good, and for it to be good, composers have to have well-developed craft skills, and for that to happen there has to be good teaching and open-minded listening.

What has emerged from this study is a strong sense that there are threads of common purpose across the stylistic spectrum. Any number, if not all, of the works discussed here could have been included in sections of the book other than those where they appeared: Ross Edwards and Paul Stanhope could have been included in 'The Place of Spirit', Elena Kats-Chernin in 'The Tyranny of Dissonance?', and so on. Edwards, Michael Smetanin and Liza Lim all contemplate the heavens in very different musics; Georges Lentz, pursuing a spiritual vision in highly abstract 'European' language, nonetheless finds himself in the world of Sculthorpe's *irkanda*, a lonely place, from which we might hope the prophets still come.

I won't say the future for live music is rosy, at a time when for many organisations the bottom line is the 'bum on the seat', and talk of key performance indicators (KPIs) and benchmarks takes precedence over artistic vision. On the other hand, music is much more accessible than it was a few decades ago: since Covell's book we have had the rise of FM broadcasting and, more recently, the Web, which makes it possible to disseminate music in a previously unimaginable way. For instance, ABC Classic FM's Australian Music Unit began uploading broadcast recordings of significant Australian works to its website in late 2008; commercial recordings are, similarly, becoming increasingly available in live audio streaming. For a small population spread over a huge landmass we can be proud of the number and quality of our composers and performers, and their presence on both the domestic and international stage. With the help of engaged and enthusiastic listeners we'll do even better. Johann Friedrich Reichardt was wrong: you can't have too much of a good – and even more of a strong – thing.

CD Contents

Many of the works discussed in this book are available on CD or streaming audio as detailed elsewhere. This sampler CD gives a range of examples of recent work showing Australian music's variety. It also introduces some lesser-known works and composers.

Track 1

Georges Lentz: 'Lumen de lumine: Rho Ophiuchi' Part 2b of *Caeli enarrant ... III*
Ensemble 24, Matthew Coorey
Naxos 8.557019

Lentz's music is a deeply personal meditation on the nature of things cosmic. *Caeli enarrant...* takes its title from Psalm 19 ('The heavens are telling ...'). This work shows his distinctive sound world and mastery of string timbre.

Track 2

David Lumsdaine: 'After sunrise' from *Cambewarra Mountain*
TP 083

Much of David Lumsdaine's concert music includes representation of Australian birdsong. Here he hoes into the field, and composes an exquisite work with the raw material.

Track 3

Paul Stanhope: 'Dawn Wail for the Dead' from *Songs for the Shadowland*
Margaret Schindler, soprano

Southern Cross Soloists
4MBS10

This is a beautiful and moving lament, setting poetry by Oodgeroo Noonuccal.

Track 4

Ann Ghandar: *Rain*
Renate Turrini, piano
003

Ann Ghandar is a fine pianist herself, and has a wonderful sensitivity for the instrument's capabilities. This is one of many small, highly evocative works.

Track 5

Nigel Butterley: 'Canzona' from *Goldengrove* excerpt
Melbourne Symphony Orchestra, Isaiah Jackson
ABC Classics 446 478-2

The themes of this slow movement from the suite *Goldengrove* came to the composer when his partner was in intensive care after a serious road accident. Its title comes from a poem by Gerard Manley

Hopkins about the inevitability
of loss.

Track 6

Elena Kats-Chernin: *Tast-En* excerpt
Lisa Moore, piano
TP 040

Another fine pianist, Kats-Chernin
composed *Tast-En* (German for
keyboard) to explore the full range
of keyboard sonority, including the
sublime.

Track 7

Andrew Ford: A reel, a fling and
ghostly galliard excerpt
Grainger Quartet
ABC Classic FM recording

Ford is an example of an Australian composer whose assimilation
of his previous (British) heritage is
never nostalgic, as you'll hear.

Track 8

Don Banks: Horn Trio final move-
ment
John Harding, violin; Hector
McDonald, horn; Ian Munro piano
TP 114

Don Banks died before the period
covered in detail in this book, but in
so many ways he made that period
possible. A tireless worker as teacher
and Chair of the Music Board, he
was also one of the most important composers this country has
produced.

Track 9

Barry Conyngham: 'Velocity' from
Southern Cross
Robert Davidovici, violin; Tamás
Ungár, piano; Geoffrey Simon,
conductor
CACD1008

In *Southern Cross* Barry Conyngham contemplates the vastness of
this country and the brilliance of its
night sky.

Track 10

Michael Smetanin: *Micrographia*
Schoenberg Ensemble
Ger de Zeeuw, Joey Marijs,
percussionists; Reinbert de Leeuw,
conductor.
Radio, VPRO http://www.vpro.nl
recording

Having studied in the Netherlands, Smetanin has maintained
contacts there. This work, written
for Holland's Schoenberg Ensemble,
shows his music's characteristic
energy – especially in the marimba
solo.

Track 11

Carl Vine: Symphony No. 3 excerpt
Sydney Symphony Orchestra, Stuart
Challender
ABC Classics 426 995-2

The third of Vine's seven symphonies is a large-scale exploration of
gorgeous orchestral sound, especially
in its final pages.

Further Reading

Adorno, Theodor W, *Philosophy of Modern Music*, translated by Anne G
Mitchell & Wesley V Blomster (New York: The Seabury Press, 1973)

Broadstock, Brenton (ed), *Sound Ideas* (Sydney: Australian Music Centre,
1995)

Buzacott, Martin, *The Rite of Spring: 75 Years of ABC Music-making* (Sydney:
ABC Books, 2007)

Callaway, Frank & Tunley, David (eds), *Australian Composition in the
Twentieth Century* (Melbourne: Oxford University Press, 1978)

Covell, Roger, *Australia's Music: Themes of a New Society* (Melbourne: Sun
Books, 1967)

Ford, Andrew, *Illegal Harmonies: Music in the Twentieth Century* (Sydney: Hale
& Iremonger, 1997)

— *Composer to Composer: Conversations about Contemporary Music* (Sydney:
Allen & Unwin, 1993)

— *Dots on the Landscape* (<http://www.abc.net.au/classic/dots/>)

Glennon, James, *Australian Music and Musicians* (Adelaide: Rigby, 1968)

Hannan, Michael, *Peter Sculthorpe: His Music and Ideas 1929–1979* (Brisbane:
University of Queensland Press, 1982)

Jenkins, John & Linz, Rainer, *Arias: Recent Australian Music Theatre*
(Melbourne: Red House, 1997)

Jenkins, John, *22 Contemporary Australian Composers* (Melbourne: NMA,
1988) available online at <http://www.rainerlinz.net/NMA/22CAC/TOC.
html>

Murdoch, James, *Australia's Contemporary Composers* (Melbourne: Macmillan,
1972/ Melbourne: Sun Books, 1975)

— *Handbook of Australian Music* (Melbourne: Sun Books, 1983)

— *Peggy Glanville-Hicks: A Transposed Life* (Hillsdale, NY: Pendragon, 2002)

Richards, Fiona (ed), *The Soundscapes of Australia: Music, Place and Spirituality*
(Aldershot: Ashgate, 2007)

Rowley, Caitlin (ed), *Australia: Exploring the Musical Landscape* (Sydney:
Australian Music Centre, 1998)

Said, Edward, *Orientalism: Western Conceptions of the Orient* (Harmondsworth:

Penguin, 1991)

Sametz, Phillip, *Play On! Sixty Years of Music-making with the Sydney Symphony Orchestra* (Sydney: ABC Books, 1992/2001)

Sitsky, Larry, *Australian Piano Music of the Twentieth Century* (Westport: Praeger, 2005)

Skinner, Graeme, *Peter Sculthorpe: The Making of an Australian Composer* (Sydney: UNSW Press, 2007)

Thonell, Judy (ed), *Poles Apart: The Music of Roger Smalley* (Perth: Evos Music; Nedlands: CIRCME, 1994)

List of Discussed Works

Commercially available recordings of works discussed in detail

Record catalogues are by nature ephemeral, especially for a relatively small niche like contemporary classical music. Some of the CD titles listed below may be difficult to find in record shops, but the good news is that an ever-increasing number can be found online. At the time of writing, the majority of ABC Classics recordings listed here could be found in the Naxos Music Library and/or iTunes store; the smaller labels are on track to begin uploading their material soon.

Edwards, Ross: *Star Chant*
Symphony No. 1 and Symphony No. 4
Adelaide Symphony Orchestra, conductor Richard Mills
ABC Classics 476 6161

Finsterer, Mary: *Omaggio alla Pietá*
on *Catch*
Various artists
ABC Classics 476 176-0

Henderson, Moya & Rodriguez, Judith: *Lindy: Opera in 2 Acts*
Opera Australia
ABC Classics 476 7489

Kats-Chernin, Elena: *Mythic*
on *Wild Swans*
Tasmanian Symphony Orchestra
ABC Classics 476 7639

Koehne, Graeme: *Elevator Music*
on *Inflight Entertainment*

Diana Doherty oboe, Sydney Symphony Orchestra, conductor Takua Yuasa
NAXOS 8.555847

Lentz, Georges: *Caeli enarrant … III & IV; Birrung; Ngurraa*
Ensemble 24, conductor Matthew Coorey
Naxos 8.557019

Lumsdaine, David: *Mandala V*
on *Hagoromo and other orchestra; works*
West Australian Symphony Orchestra, conductor Diego Masson, Albert Rosen
ABC Classics 426 994-2

Meale, Richard & Malouf, David: *Voss*
Geoffrey Chard, Marilyn Richardson
The Australian Opera, Sydney Symphony Orchestra
ABC Classics 420 928-2

Schultz, Andrew & Williams, Gordon Kalton: *Journey to Horseshoe Bend:
A Cantata Based on the Novel by TGH Strehlow*
Aaron Pedersen, John Stanton, Rodney Macann, Ntaria Ladies Choir,
Sydney Philharmonia Choirs; Sydney Symphony Orchestra, conductor
David Porcelijn
ABC Classics 476 2266

Sculthorpe, Peter: *Mangrove*
on *Songs of Sea and Sky*
Queensland Orchestra, conductor Michael Christie
ABC Classics 476 192-1

Smalley: *Diptych – Homage to Brian Blanchflower*
on *Forbidden Colours: Orchestral music by Smalley, Formosa, Brophy and Kos*
Melbourne Symphony Orchestra conductors Gunther Schuller, Patrick
Thomas; Queensland Symphony Orchestra conductors Myer Fredman,
John Hopkins
VAST015-2

Vine, Carl: *Piano Sonata No. 1*
on *Chamber Music vol. 2*
Performers include Michael Kieran Harvey, Geoffrey Collins, David Miller,
the Tall Poppies Quartet, Ian Munro, David Pereira
TP 120

Also recommended

Boyd, Anne: *As I crossed a bridge of dreams*
on *Crossing a bridge of dreams*
Various performers
TP 127

Butterley, Nigel: *From Sorrowing Earth*
Melbourne Symphony Orchestra, conductor Isaiah Jackson
ABC Classics 446 487-2

Chisholm, David: *Origami*
Silo Quartet
MD 3307

Conyngham, Barry: *Southern Cross* and *Monuments*
Robert Davidovici, violin; Tamás Ungár, piano
London Symphony Orchestra, conductor Geoffrey Simon
CACD1008

Dean, Brett: *Beggars and Angels*
Melbourne Symphony Orchestra, conductor Markus Stenz
ABC Classics 476 160-6

Lim, Liza: *The Heart's Ear*
Performers include Ensemble Modern and Elision
ABC Classics 456 687-2

Wesley-Smith, Martin & Peter: *Quito – A documentary music-drama about schizo-phrenia and East Timor*
Featuring The Song Company
TP 111

Compilations and anthologies

A Patchwork of Shadows
Includes music of Malcolm Williamson, Gordon Kerry, Keith Humble, Peter Sculthorpe, Roger Smalley, Katharine Parker
Ian Munro, piano
TP 058

Australian Cello
Includes music by Don Banks, Keith Humble, Bozidar Kos, Gillian
Whitehead
Georg Pedersen, cello, David Bollard, piano
TP 129

Australian Violin Concertos: Nigel Butterley, Don Banks, Margaret Sutherland
Leonard Dommett, violin
Tasmanian Symphony Orchestra, conductor Wilfred Lehmann; Melbourne
Symphony Orchestra, conductor Patrick Thomas
ABC Classics 426 993-2

From Rags to Recollections; Australian Piano Music
Includes music by Elena Kats-Chernin, Ann Ghandar, Beverley Lea, Gordon
Kerry, Peter Sculthorpe, Alistair Noble and John Welch
Renate Turrini, piano
003

Illegal Harmonies
Includes music by Percy Grainger, Anne Boyd, Elena Kats-Chernin (also
Satie, Ravel, Joplin, Debussy, Schoenberg, Stravinsky, Gershwin, Messiaen,
Cage, Stockhausen, Young, Berio, Copland, Ligeti, Pärt, Takemitsu)
Stephanie McCallum, piano
ABC Classics 456 6682

Samsara
Includes music by Larry Sitsky, Gordon Kerry, Don Banks, Bozidar Kos,
Carl Vine
Australia Ensemble
VAST020-2

Southern Cross Soloists: Australia
Includes music by Paul Stanhope, Roy Agnew, Mary Mageau, Alison Bauld,
Dulcie Holland, Richard Mills, Gordon Kerry, Stephen Stanfield, Vincent
Plush
4MBS10

Strange Attractions
Includes music by Michael Smetanin, Michael Finnissy, Mary Finsterer,
Helen Gifford, Liza Lim, Anne Boyd and David Lumsdaine

Sydney Alpha Ensemble
ABC Classics 456 537-2

Stroke
Includes music by Michael Smetanin, Don Banks, Elena Kats-Chernin,
Julian Yu, Andrew Ford, Ross Edwards, Gerard Brophy, Peter Sculthorpe,
Martin Wesley-Smith
Lisa Moore, piano
TP 040

Tasmanian Symphony Orchestra: Australian Composer series
Vol. 1: 5 CDs featuring Carl Vine, Ross Edwards, Nigel Westlake, Gordon
Kerry, Richard Mills
ABC Classics 476 5698

Tasmanian Symphony Orchestra: Australian Composer series
Vol. 2: 5 CDs featuring Peter Sculthorpe, Elena Kats-Chernin, Brenton
Broadstock, Larry Sitsky, Don Kay
ABC Classics 476 5699

Tasmania Symphony / Sinfonia da Pacifica
Includes music by Don Kay and Peggy Glanville-Hicks
Tasmanian Symphony Orchestra, conductor Richard Mills
VAST013-2

Toward the Shining Light – Orchestral works by Conyngham, Broadstock and Banks
Melbourne Symphony Orchestra, conductor Richard Mills
ABC Classics 426 807-2

Woman's Song: Australian Settings of Judith Wright
Music by Sutherland, Edwards, Mills, Munro, Henderson
Elizabeth Campbell, mezzo-soprano
Ian Munro, piano
TP 179

Notes

Introduction

1   Much quoted in the Beethoven literature, but see HC Robbins Landon: *Beethoven: His Life, Work and World* (London: Thames & Hudson, 1992), p. 149.

Chapter 1

1   James Murdoch: *Australia's Contemporary Composers* (Melbourne: Macmillan, 1972/ Melbourne: Sun Books, 1975).

Chapter 2

1   William Dampier's 1688 account is anthologised in Tim Flannery: *The Explorers* (Melbourne: Text, 1998) p. 28.

2   Wagner's letter is reproduced as an illustration in John Cargher: *Opera and Ballet in Australia* (Stanmore: Cassell Australia, 1977).

3   John Mansfield Thomson: *A Distant Music: The Life and Times of Alfred Hill 1870–1960* (Auckland: Oxford University Press, 1980) p. 211.

4   Ibid., p. 225.

5   Grainger is the subject of numerous books and articles. See John Bird's biography *Percy Grainger* (Currency Press, 1998); Malcolm Gillies & Bruce Clunies Ross (eds): *Grainger on Music* (Oxford University Press, 1999).

Chapter 3

1   Email from the composer to the author, 12 April 2008.

2   Quoted in Gordon Kerry, 'To be alone' in Fiona Richards (ed): *The Soundscapes of Australia* (Aldershot: Ashgate, 2007) p. 251.

3   Quoted in Harry Heseltine, 'Australian Fiction since 1920' in Geoffrey Dutton (ed): *The Literature of Australia* (Melbourne: Penguin, 1964), p. 210.

4   David Malouf's libretto to *Voss* is reprinted in the discography, The Australian Opera, Sydney Symphony Orchestra, ABC Classics 420928-2, 1987, by permission of Boosey and Hawkes (Australia).

5   SATB: soprano, alto, tenor and bass.

Chapter 4

1   Knopoff is based at the Elder Conservatorium, University of Adelaide. He has contributed to numerous scholarly journals, the Australian Music Centre's *Sounds Australian* (now *Resonate*) magazine and the *New Grove Dictionary of Music and Musicians*.

2   Composer's program note available at his website: <www.rogersmalley.com>

3   Program note available on Colin Bright's website <brightmusic.net>

4   David Tacey: *Edge of the Sacred* (Melbourne: HarperCollins, 1995) p. 135.

5   Richard Taruskin: *The Oxford History of Western Music* (New York: Oxford University Press, 2005) vol. 6, p. 526.

6   <http://www.abc.net.au/classic/dots/>

7   Liner notes for *Strange Attractions*, ABC Classics 456 537-2.

8   Lim's remarks quoted throughout are from an interview with the author in March 2006.

Chapter 5

1   Richard Mills' program note to *Bamaga Diptych*, 1989.

2   I am using the term 'post-modern' to denote an approach to art which makes self-conscious and often ironic use of its own artifice. This often includes reference to previously existing styles or works, and is thus in direct opposition to Modernism in music with its insistence on the autonomy of the work.

3   Sculthorpe retails this story in his autobiography *Sun Music: Journeys and Reflections from a Composer's Life* (Sydney: ABC Books, 1999) p. 275.

4   Graeme Skinner: *Peter Sculthorpe: The Making of an Australian Composer* (Sydney: UNSW Press, 2007).

5   This and the previous quotation are from the program note for *Mangrove*, 1979.

6   Michael Hannan: *Peter Sculthorpe: His Music and Ideas 1929–1979* (Brisbane: University of Queensland Press, 1982) pp. 195–98.

7   Liner notes of *Lake Emu* CD, TP092 (1996).

8   Program note for *Mandala V*, 1988.

9   Significantly, the image is also crucial to Patrick White's seventh novel *The Solid Mandala* published in 1966.

10   Notes to *Hagoromo: Orchestral Works*, ABC Classics 426994-2 (1990).

11   James McAuley, 'Terra Australis' in *Collected Poems* (Melbourne: Angus & Robertson, 1978).

12   Email from the composer to the author 7 June 2008.

13   Ibid.

14   Composer's program note to *Mandala V*, 1988.

Chapter 6

1   See Edward Said: *Orientalism: Western Conceptions of the Orient* (Harmondsworth: Penguin, 1991).

2   Notes to Contemporary Australian Piano Music, LP VRL1-0083.

3   Composer's program note to *Thousands of Bundled Straw*, 2005.

4   See Gordon Kerry, 'To be alone' in Fiona Richards (ed): *Soundscapes of Australia*, (Aldershot: Ashgate, 2007).

5   Program note for *Afterimages*, 1994.

6   Yukio Mishima: *The Temple of the Golden Pavilion*, translated Ivan Morris (London: Penguin, 1987), p. 53.

7   Program note to *The Temple of the Golden Pavilion*, 1979.

Chapter 7

1   Sitsky's remarks can be heard at <http://www.abc.net.au/classic/dots>

2   David Osmond-Smith, 'Donatoni' in Stanley Sadie (ed): *The New Grove Dictionary of Music and Musicians*, (London: Macmillan,

2001), p. 461.

3   Program notes to *Cries and Whispers*, 1993.

4   Composer's program note to *Dispersal*, 2001.

5   Maynard Solomon: *Mozart: A Life* (London: Hutchinson, 1995), p. 378.

6   Material quoted in this section and extended notes are available on the composer's website at <www.curiousnoise.com>

Chapter 8

1   Quoted in James Murdoch: *Peggy Glanville-Hicks: A Transposed Life* (Hillsdale, NY: Pendragon, 2002), p. 71.

2   See Larry Sitsky: *Australian Piano Music of the Twentieth Century* (Westport: Praeger, 2005).

3   From a letter to the author, quoted in Gordon Kerry 'Keeping live music alive' in *Musica Viva Australia: The First Fifty Years* (Sydney: Playbill, 1996).

4   Program note to the String Quartet No. 2, 1980.

5   Interview with Andrew Ford on ABC Radio National's *The Music Show*, 6 September 2003. See <http://www.abc.net.au/rn/musicshow/stories/2003/964163.htm>

6   Program note to *Inflight Entertainment*, 2000.

7   Program note to *Elevator Music*, 1997.

8   Interview with Andrew Ford on ABC Radio National's *The Music Show*, 16 August 2003. See <http://www.abc.net.au/rn/musicshow/stories/2003/932436.htm>

9   Program note to Symphony No. 1, 1991.

10   See <http://www.abc.net.au/rn/spiritofthings/stories/2006/1673006.htm>

11   Program note to Symphony No. 2, 1998.

12   For further discussion on the Federation bells, see the section on the work of Constantine Koukias later in this book.

13   Program note to Symphony No. 4, 2002.

14   See <http://www.abc.net.au/rn/spiritofthings/stories/2006/1673006.htm>

15   Program note to '*My song is love unknown*', 2000.

16   See the composer's website at <www.paulstanhope.com>

Chapter 9

1   Quoted in Mark Coughlan, 'From west to east' in *Resonate* magazine, 31 July 2007 <http://www.resonatemagazine.com.au/article.php?id=6>

2   This and the following quotes relating to the composition are from the composer's program note for *Diptych*, 1991.

3   TS Eliot, 'East Coker' from *Four Quartets: Collected Poems* (London: Faber & Faber, 1964).

4   See <http://www.holmesacourtgallery.com.au/collection/artist-profile.cfm?artist_id=52>

5   Program note for *On Canaan's Happier Shore*, 1985, available at the composer's website at <www.andrewford.net.au>

6   Quoted in Andrew Ford: *Illegal Harmonies: Music in the Twentieth*

Century (Sydney: Hale & Iremonger, 1997), p. 252.

Chapter 10

1 Gisela Rothe (ed (compiler)): *Recorders Based on Historical Models: Fred Morgan – Writings and Memories* (Fulda: Mollenhauer, 2007). See also <www.mollenhauer.com>

2 <http://www.aamim.org.au/>

3 Michael Hannan: *The Australian Guide to Careers in Music* (Sydney: UNSW Press, 2003), p. 120.

4 See especially Theodor W Adorno: *Philosophy of Modern Music*, translated by Anne G Mitchell &Wesley V Blomster (New York: The Seabury Press, 1973) for his articulation of the serialism versus tonality debate.

5 This and the following quotes are from the composer's program notes to *Mysterium cosmographicum*, premiered with the Sydney Symphony Orchestra, 2005.

6 Composer's program note to the Seventh Symphony, for the first performance by the West Australian Symphony Orchestra, 2008.

Chapter 11

1 CD liner note to *Strange Attractions*, ABC Classics 456 537-2.

2 *The Famous History of the Life of King Henry VIII* or, *All That is True* by William Shakespeare (possibly co-written by John Fletcher), 1623.

3 David Garrett: program note to *Heaven is Closed*, 2000.

4 Composer's program note, 2004.

5 See for instance his *Wagner's 'Ring' and its Symbols* (New York:

St Martins, 1963) or *Opera and its Symbols* (New Haven: Yale University Press, 1991).

6 'Philomele' is a more direct transliteration of the original Greek than Ovid's Latinised version; in *A Midsummer Night's Dream*, Shakespeare uses the form 'Philomel'.

Chapter 12

1 Transcript of interview with Andrew Ford on *The Music Show*, ABC Radio National, <www.abc.net.au/rn/musicshow/stories/2005/1315401.htm>

2 Email to the author from Elizabeth Barcan, 2 June 2008.

3 See <www.ausbell.com>

4 *Sacrosanctum Concilium* (Constitution on the sacred liturgy, 1963), Chapter VI.

5 Christopher Willcock's program note to *Gospel Bestiary*, 2000.

6 'Uncial' refers to the script used in the early Middle Ages, characterised by neatly rounded letters produced with one stroke of the pen on vellum or parchment.

7 CD liner notes to *Catch*, ABC Classics 476 176-0.

8 Ibid.

9 Composer's program note to *Ascension and Descend*, 2001.

10 Traherne's prose-cycle, *Centuries of Meditations*, was first published only in 1908, more than two centuries after his death.

11 Elliott Gyger's program note for Butterley's *Spell of Creation*, 2000.

12 All quotations in this section are from the composer's website <www.georgeslentz.com>

Index

For Jeffrey

A UNSW Press book

Published by
University of New South Wales Press Ltd
University of New South Wales
Sydney NSW 2052
AUSTRALIA
www.unswpress.com.au

© Gordon Kerry 2009
First published 2009

National Library of Australia
Cataloguing-in-Publication entry
Author: Gordon, Kerry.
Title: New classical music: composing Australia/Gordon Kerry.
ISBN: 978 086840 983 2 (pbk.)
Subjects: Composition (Music)
          Composers − Australia.
Dewey Number: 780.994

Design Josephine Pajor-Markus
Printer Everbest, China

This book is printed on paper using fibre supplied from plantation or sustainably managed
forests.

This project is supported by the Australia Council, the Australian Government's arts funding
and advisory body, through its Music Board Section.

Australian Government

Australia **Council**
for the Arts